The True-Life Adventures of Genie and Janny: An American Original and his Faithful Corporal at Arms

By Janny Vaughan

Edited by Danielle DeConcilio

TM

The True-Life Adventures of Genie and Janny: An American Original and his Faithful Corporal at Arms
Copyright © 2010 by Janet Vaughan.

Drawings by Tina Hagstrom.

The author expresses her appreciation to The Johnny Mercer Foundation for permission to reprint of Johnny Mercer's song titles and lyrics, which are copyrighted, as follows:

Too Marvelous For Words:	©1937 (Music by Richard Whiting)
Accentuate the Positive:	©1944 (Music by Harold Arlen)
And the Angels Sing:	©1939 (Music by Ziggy Elman)
Glow Worm:	©1952 (Music by Paul Lincke)
I Remember You:	©1942

All rights reserved. No part of this book may be used or reproduced in any manner whatsoever without written permission of the Author.

ISBN 978-1-456-37591-1

Printed and bound in the United States of America.

This book is dedicated to my compatriot and beloved brother, Dewey Eugene Hall, a.k.a. Genie.

Genie, in his wise and wonderful gift of mind and spirit, understood if children everywhere were allowed their full measure of childhood, to dream dreams adults find difficult to imagine and to entertain "fantasy" as a respected part of growing up, then "This old world will renew itself over and over again until the end of time . . .until all the forever's . . .and just maybe, the children will let us know . . .what comes after . . . ."

Table of Contents

Foreword

Chapter 1: The Killing of Big Red

Chapter 2: Dewey Eugene Hall/Genie

Chapter 3: Hard Times

Chapter 4: Old Molly

Chapter 5: The Whipping

Chapter 6: Baby Ducks and Lilacs

Chapter 7: Sergeant Major Calico

Chapter 8: The "Old Ones"

Chapter 9: Geronimo and the Last Snowball

Chapter 10: A Cow Named Reddy

Chapter 11: The Second Star to the Right . . .

Chapter 12: Even Angels Die

Epilogue: "Plan A" Completed, Sir

Afterword

Acknowledgments

Foreword

When you're young, the world isn't limited by the boundaries of reality or time. Days may be endless and nights filled with starships, wishes, and unicorns to ride. The imagination every child is born with dances in the moonlight to songs only children hear. A child's sense of truth may differ from an adult's. A child's truth can't always be proven, but it can be lived and faithfully documented by the heart's journey. Upon these pages, you'll find such a journey, a journey to the end of childhood and to the beginning of memories, memories that will last forever. Hang on, Genie; this is "Plan A," bearing all my love . . . .

Dear Karen,

I hope my book will lift your spirits and make smiles upon your heart.

My brother was truly a remarkable human being and I miss him every day of my life —

Blue Skies — always

Jonny

2011

Chapter One:
The Killing of Big Red

"Hit the dirt, soldier," shouted the Captain.

"Yes, Sir," I answered smartly, dropping knees to belly, crawling on all fours as fast as I could while balancing my wooden rifle between the crook of my arms, safe from the revolting mess directly beneath me—the smell of which was about to do me in.

"Sir?"

"Yes, Corporal."

"Sir, I wish to report this stuff, that is, this mess, Sir, is really awful. I'm not sure I can make it through, Sir. All due respect, Sir."

"Corporal Hall?"

"Yes, Sir."

"Listen up, soldier, and listen good! This is no chicken-shit detail: this is important duty. Keep moving forward until you have the objective in sight. Is that clear, Corporal?"

"Yes, Sir," came my choked reply, as I thought, *Don't tell me this isn't chicken-shit when I'm belly deep in it.* Never, under any circumstances, would I have disobeyed my Captain, whom I trusted with life and limb, and admired with fierce pride and unceasing loyalty (rather like a dog to his master), if you know what I mean. Besides, the Captain was my brother.

In my brief life as a soldier, mercenary, slave, and all around GI Joe, I had gone on countless maneuvers with this Lone Ranger, as I sometimes referred to my Captain. These operations included night raids into enemy territory, jumping off roofs, riding wild horses and the occasional cow, and swinging from a rope 100-feet in the air over the concrete floor in our Grandfather's barn. This is to say nothing of swimming the Rhine, which in fact was our creek, digging foxholes with my bare hands, or eating wild onions, potatoes, and apples from our orchard. I was a terrific scrounger and had managed to survive anything and everything, until now.

I could feel my stomach beginning to reject the sweet cider from my canteen, and I was in dire need of a clothespin for my nose. While the cider was on the rise, I peered into the murky light of an ancient egg warmer and spotted the objective, our repugnant enemy—a hulk of bone, feathers, and pure evil sound asleep in the midst of his favorite plumed ladies.

"Sir," I whispered excitedly, "I see him, Sir." My Captain perched on a high stool, clean and secure by the door, aimed his flashlight in the direction of my voice. "Over there, Sir, to your right."

"Yes, I see him now, Corporal. Good work."

"Thank you, Sir."

"Now, Corporal, get your rope untied and place the prisoner in lock up. Be quick and be silent."

"Right, Sir." My Captain referred to the rope that was tied around my left ankle and attached to a large galvanized tin tub I had been dragging along behind me for what seemed like miles. I untied the rope, rose to my knees, stood up, leaned down, and picked up the tub, holding it over my head as I began to move inch by inch into harms way.

"Corporal Hall, do you remember your orders?"

"Yes, Sir."

"Then commence on the count of three: one, two, *three*!" In one great heroic dash, I slammed the tub down hard over Big Red and his ladies of the night, catching them off guard. I immediately sat down hard on the tub, breathing a huge sigh of relief.

"Corporal Hall, is the prisoner secure?"

"Yes, Sir, so long as I keep sitting on top of this tin tub."

"Excellent, Corporal. I'm placing you in complete charge of the prisoner until I pronounce sentence at dawn. You are to maintain your position until 0600, understood?"

"S-sir," I stammered, "Sir, are you telling me to sit on this tin tub all night, alone, in the middle of all this chicken-shit, uh, sorry Sir, in this mess, in the dark, Sir?"

"Corporal, need I remind you that Marines are not, I repeat, *not* afraid of the dark, understood?"

"Yes, Sir."

"Remember, Corporal, chicken coop, brig, pokey, it's all the same. This is a dangerous prisoner and he is your responsibility until you are relieved. Now, sit on it, Corporal; that's an order! Do not let me down. Remember the Corps, Corporal: Semper Fi."

"Yes, Sir, I'll remember, Sir." I said with as much esprit de corps as I could muster. I heard my Captain exit most certainly to a warm bed and a mug of hot chocolate, and I will tell you the honest truth, here and now, the life of a soldier is not an easy one and if, like me, your Captain is your big brother, then you had better BEWARE because at some point in time, you will find yourself up to your ears in you-know-what, from God knows where, and from God knows who.

This was the worst detail I was ever assigned. It was to be an annihilation of the first order, but well deserved, I can assure you. The prisoner, Big Red, as he was called, had already had his trial and been convicted. The evidence was overwhelming, crystal clear, and non-refutable. All that remained was the sentencing. What you need to know is that Big Red was guilty beyond a shadow of a doubt. His fate was sealed and severe action had to be taken. After all, Big Red had been given countless chances to turn his life around. Instead, he continued in his unprecedented, horrendous killing spree. Tiny bodies of baby kittens, chicks, ducklings, rabbits, even several little white fleecy barn owls littered the yard, day in and day out. There was mass hysteria, clucking, and the flapping of wings. It was clear for anyone to see . . .Big Red was a psychopath.

Big Red actually enjoyed killing. He was now Public Enemy Number One, Jack the Ripper, and Attila the Hun all rolled into one. Big Red was a high-steppin', crowing dandy, a swaggering bully, adorned from head to foot with long, silky feathers of royal blue, green, indigo, black and, of course, the deep crimson color of blood. My brother took one look at Big Red on the day he arrived and said, "To look into those eyes is to see death staring back at you." The die was cast: Big Red had to go.

The year was 1943 and the place a seedy, ramshackle 40-acre farm in Grant County, Indiana. We were Hoosiers and proud of it. Farmers grew corn, kids played basketball, and most folks went to church on Sundays. Everybody was involved in the war effort, which involved planting Victory Gardens, collecting tin and rubber, and using tokens for meat, bread, and milk. Even kids collected foil from inside cigarette packs. Mom, Dad, and Grandpa all smoked Luckies. Lucky Strikes were the best because Lucky Strikes went to war. Everybody knew that, especially my brother, Genie, who was totally obsessed by anything concerning the war.

Genie was my mentor, my Captain, my omniscient one because Genie knew everything about everything. He was dead sure the dreaded Nazis would attack and try to capture our Grandparent's farm. This attack could come at any time, and it was up to us to protect the farm and every living thing on it. It was to this grand end that he devoted himself completely and me right along with him. Since he was too young to join up, he created his own private Army Reserve Marine Corps.

I was to have a most important role in this Army because, you see, the rest of the Army, after my brother, was me! I was the private, Corporal, cook, medic, runner, radioman, lookout, platoon leader, and the entire platoon itself. The others in our Army were referred to as the Silent Militia. This group consisted of three cows, Old Molly (our horse), Miss Lucy (my pet duck), numerous chickens, Calico cat, our dogs Bruno and Spot, and various and sundry animals that came and went on our 40 acres. Grandma and Grandpa Nelson, who didn't know they had been inducted into the Corps, nevertheless became invaluable. You could count on them above and beyond their call of duty.

My brother, Genie, was one smart kid. I've already mentioned he knew everything about everything, and if he didn't, he'd quickly read up on it. Genie probably read more books than anyone in the whole wide world. If it was printed on paper, Genie read it. He read three or four books a night. Genie even had a
book about Hitler but told me not to tell anyone, ever, and I never did.

Everyone in our house listened to the news on the radio. Our family ate, slept, and memorized every word Franklin Delano Roosevelt said to the American people. Dad said we should know about what was going on "over there." Our father respected and trusted F.D.R. and Mom loved Eleanor like a sister. Our Grandparents felt the same, as they were part of our family. As far as I was concerned, if Genie stamped his okay on this, then it was good enough for me. Besides, I thought it was pretty nice for a busy president to take time out to read the Sunday funnies to his citizens.

Genie had drawn up complicated and detailed war plans on how to fight off the fiendish Nazis should they parachute onto our farm. He had made up passwords and special code speaking, which was a closely guarded secret, punished by a fate worse than death: another year in Genie's Army! Sitting there in the half-dark, on top of the cold galvanized tub, breathing in 98% pure nitrogen, it came to me that I could die right here at checkpoint 4, known to civilians as the chicken coop. I wondered how this war and Big Red were connected, and as I thought about the dastardly deeds Big Red had committed, it dawned on me that Big Red would have been sworn into the Third Reich instantly. After all, Big Red had no heart, was devoid of conscience, loved to kill, and was extremely arrogant; in short, Big Red was the perfect Nazi.

From the first moment big Red stepped into our barnyard, his final curtain was drawn. Big Red was the result of one of Grandpa's infamous trades. What must be explained here, and very reluctantly, is the fact our beloved Grandpa, Clyde Guy Nelson, was the worst farmer in the state of Indiana, or any other state for that matter. It wasn't his fault: he had never been a farmer nor ever desired to be a farmer. Circumstances quite beyond his control had set his feet onto soil.

Grandpa had worked as a coal miner in Pennsylvania, an oil rigger in Oklahoma, a fruit picker in Washington State, and a cowhand in Kansas. He hauled pigs out of Ohio and became a rodeo roust-about at the Indiana State Fair. Before coming to the farm, he worked for Paranite Wire and Cable Company located in Marion, Indiana. Marion was where Genie and I lived with our folks and went to school, but when summer came, we headed for the farm and spent all three months in the place we loved best.

Grandma and Grandpa Nelson were there to take care of Grandma's ailing mother, Jenny Thomas. Jenny was 83 or 85—no one knew for sure—and her husband, Will Thomas, was close to being 100-years-old, and stood 6'6" with a huge shock of pure white hair. We didn't know much about them, except it was plain to see that Jenny Thomas was a mean, bitter old woman who daily cursed and damned the world and everyone in it, especially our beloved Grandma. Will was crazy as a bedbug and meaner than sin. He loved chasing after us with a double-barreled shotgun, which the grownups thought didn't work, but in fact, did. Genie and I had no love for either of them and we called them the "The Old Ones."

Grandpa Nelson had a great big heart of gold, that's number one. The second best thing about him was his outstanding ability to tell a story. Everyone said Grandpa was right up there with Mark Twain, Herb Shriner, and of course, our father. However, none of these aforementioned men could cuss like Grandpa. I know it may not sound nice to say, but Grandpa's style of cussing was a gift. People loved to hear him lay into his poetic malediction of the English language. There was no blaspheming, mind you; it was simply the pure, rancorous, headstrong vexation of a man done wrong. Words flew from his mouth neither man nor beast had ever heard before. Folks would actually gather 'round to hear our Grandpa articulate, fabricate, and generally regenerate, the spoken word. No doubt about it, Grandpa was a real honest-to-goodness character and the best Grandpa a kid could ever hope to have. He was also a pretty darn good horse trader. Deal making was his real calling. Everything living on the farm had been or was going to be a "trade." Genie and I loved it because we never knew what Grandpa might come home with next and the marvelous story which would accompany it.

One fine June day, Grandpa loaded Sam the billy goat onto the truck. Sam had recently lost favor with Grandma when he yanked her best dress, petticoat, and underwear off the clothesline and proceeded to eat them while spitting the pearl buttons at her feet. Grandma had put up with a lot from Sam, everything from eating fresh berry pies off the windowsill to chasing the preacher into the cornfield. But this time Sam had gone too far. Genie and I watched from the boughs of a cherry tree. Genie said, "I'm glad to get rid of Sam. He was the worst soldier in my unit. He would never take a direct order or stand at attention."

As Grandpa drove out the barnyard gate, we could see old Sam chewing away on the rope holding him in the truck. Genie sighed heavily, shaking his head, "I hope Grandpa makes it through enemy lines with that crack-pot Sam and is able to make a decent trade."

"Me, too," I giggled, covering my mouth so Genie couldn't hear. Late in the afternoon, Grandpa returned with a big smile on his face. Genie and I ran to the truck to see the new trade.

"Look in here, kids, and see your Grandpa's fantastic find." Genie and I peered through a slatted cage at a giant feathered hulk of a rooster.

"Ain't he something?" Grandpa asked proudly. "This here rooster is Big Red, a champion fighting rooster from Gooseneck, Tennessee. He's got papers of authenticity, yes, sir. Kids, Big Red is the real McCoy." We could tell Grandpa was extremely happy with this trade. Genie and I smiled and watched as Grandpa opened the cage and let Big Red out. From the moment Big Red's orange feet, festooned with long razor sharp talons, hit the ground Genie had his number. Genie watched intently as Big Red strutted around the barnyard as if he alone owned it. Once or twice, he actually pawed the ground and stretched out his wings, which were at least three feet in length. Big Red was certainly impressive.

Genie quietly bent down and whispered in my ear, "Janny, I want you to stay away from Big Red. Grandpa's gone and got himself a sure-fire psycho rooster. God, help us."

I knew Genie knew everything about everything, so I figured he must have read a book on the life and times of a psycho rooster. As it turned out, Genie was dead right about Big Red. Any living thing that dared cross the barnyard was subject to attack. The hens were terrified of him. He pounced on them regularly without warning. Afterward, they would stagger away, feathers falling, to seek refuge under the nearest lilac bush. Genie and I tried to tell Grandpa how dangerous Big Red really was, but he laughed saying, Big Red was just "feeling his oats!" and letting everyone know who was boss. Genie said Big Red was doing a whole lot more then merely "feeling his oats." Genie declared Big Red to be a cold-blooded monster that enjoyed the act of killing. Grandpa's answer was to say, Genie was "making a mountain out of a molehill." Genie vowed sooner or later Big Red would show his true colors and Grandpa would become a believer. That day arrived sooner than we expected.

Genie and I had been out all day on a reconnaissance mission setting out new traps for the Germans. We were lying on our bellies at checkpoint Strawberry, which was the ditch in front of the farmhouse. Checkpoint Strawberry was a favorite stop-off because its banks were brimful of wild, sweet strawberries, each the size of a dime.

"Look sharp, Corporal. Over there." Genie's command was sudden and unexpected.

"Yes, Sir," I mumbled, pulling myself up to eye-level of the fallen log I had been leaning against. What I saw froze my blood. It was Grandpa, dressed up in his one and only Sunday-go-to-meetin' suit topped off by his new gray felt hat. He was carrying large buckets of slop for the hogs, one in each hand. Directly down wind from Grandpa strutted Big Red, who had just finished having his way with a little brown hen so traumatized by the ordeal, she couldn't run for cover and stood as if nailed to the spot.

"Damn," Genie said, adding, "Corporal, get out your notebook and enter the charge of rapist to Big Red's offenses."

"What's a rapist, Sir, and how do you spell it?"

Genie gave me one of his General Patton's frowns and said, "Never mind, I'll tell you later, a lot later. Right now, our job is to warn the civilian he's in grave danger."

"You mean Grandpa?"

"Of course, Corporal, get your wits about you soldier: this could get serious." Meanwhile, Big Red was casually preening himself in the warm sunshine.

"Would you look at the beast, Corporal? He's pretending not to see Grandpa. Here's what we're going to do, on the count of three, we will commence screaming as loud as we can WATCH OUT GRANDPA!" The word *two* had just left Genie's mouth when Big Red lowered his head and actually began pawing the ground like a Spanish bull in the arena. Big Red spread his wings and lunged forward with incredible speed and took to the air; it was an awesome sight.

"Holy, Jesus!" Genie cried out, "Big Red is going to dive bomb Grandpa!" Genie and I screamed as loudly as we could. Grandpa turned his head in the direction of our voices just as Big Red smashed into his chest, cutting the Blue Serge to ribbons and knocking the breath out of Grandpa. He fell to his knees, cussing like blue blazes. As he fell, slop went everywhere but mostly on Grandpa. His hat had fallen to the ground and Big Red was pecking Grandpa's head. Blood was streaming down his face. Big Red's huge wings were like fists pummeling Grandpa's body. Grandpa covered his face with his hands and slowly sank to the ground.

Genie and I ran towards him hollering while pelting Big Red with rocks we scooped up along the way. I was completely hysterical, "Genie," I cried, "Big Red is killing Grandpa." Grandpa lay face down on the ground. Big Red was on top of Grandpa's back, ripping away at him in a non-stop pecking frenzy.

"Hang on Grandpa: we'll save you," Genie shouted. "Keep throwing those rocks, Janny. I'm going to the barn to find a weapon." In the meantime, my rocks were bouncing off Big Red as if they were rubber balls. Part of Grandpa's back was completely exposed and Big Red was going after it like it was his Sunday dinner!

"Hurry, Genie!" I screamed, "Big Red is eating Grandpa!"

"Not for long he isn't," Genie yelled as he ran by me carrying the large wooden hayfork. Somehow, he managed to hoist it up over his head and came down slugging it like a baseball bat. He struck Big Red square in his mid-section, which knocked him off Grandpa's back. But the bird scrambled up and ran for cover before Genie could hit him again. Genie dropped to his knees, throwing his slim body over Grandpa's bleeding hulk.

"Janny," Genie choked, "run to the house, get water, bandages, and the Clover Salve. Don't wake up the Old Ones, and be sure to tell Grandma that Grandpa is all right, understand?" I nodded and ran for the house. Thank my lucky stars, Big Red was nowhere in sight. I can't tell you how or why, but when I reached the back door, there stood Grandma ready with everything I needed. She told me to be careful and sent me on my way. When I reached Grandpa and Genie, to my heart's relief, Grandpa was sitting up. Boy, did he look a mess covered in cabbage leaves, potato peelings, and smelling to high heaven! He was also madder than either of us had ever seen him. Genie and I together began to wash the blood from his wounds. Most were superficial and not too deep except for the nasty hole in the left side of his head and one long, deep gash on his back. His suit was blood-soaked and in ruin. Grandpa was spewing out words like Mount Vesuvius spewing lava. Genie was doing his level best to calm him down.

Finally, Grandpa stopped shaking and was able to speak in a normal tone of voice. He put his hands on Genie's shoulders and spoke firmly in a clear and precise voice, "Genie, you are a brave lad, a strong lad, and I'm beholden to the both of you for
saving your old Grandpa's life." He shook Genie's hand and gave my pigtails a tug. "Dewey Eugene Hall, you've proved yourself to be a man today, so I'm going to ask you to do a man's job. The job will be dangerous and you will need to be extra careful and stay on your toes. Are you up for it?"

"Yes, Sir, I'm ready. What do you want me to do?"

"I want you to kill Big Red. That rooster is a menace! I want him dead before sundown tomorrow, and I don't care what you have to do to get the job done, understood?"

"Yes, Sir, Grandpa you can count on me."

"Me, too, Grandpa," I chimed in.

"Are you sure now, boy? Big Red is a bad one, the worst damn trade I ever made."

"Don't worry, Grandpa: Big Red is as good as dead. Corporal Hall and I will see to it at once."

Grandpa heaved a huge sigh of relief. "I knew I could count on you, lad, but watch yourself and Janny. Good luck." With Genie's help, Grandpa got slowly to his feet. He was unsteady, but he managed. We watched him stumble his way towards the house.

"A broken man is a hard thing to see," Genie remarked solemnly.

"Is Grandpa broken, Genie?"

"I'll explain later; right now we have to make plans. Big Red will not go down easy Janny, but by the hand of justice, he will go down!" Genie was one great speechmaker, and I believed him, without a single doubt.

It was late when we finally all sat down to dinner. Grandma had prepared Grandpa's favorite meal: fried potatoes, homemade sausage, red-eye gravy, butter beans, and hot biscuits. We noticed Grandpa didn't eat much. His right eye had begun to swell, and was turning black and blue. His lips were cut, making it hard for him to eat. Both ears looked as if they had been sliced with a razor and some of his hair was missing; he was not a pretty sight. After dinner, Grandpa went straight to bed, which meant Genie and I would miss our storytelling time. The night had turned cold and it was raining, but upstairs snug and warm under a mountain of quilts, the wheels of justice were turning 'round and 'round in Genie's mind. I could almost hear them.

As I was drifting into dreamland, Genie suddenly shouted, "Wake up, Janny! I've got the plan. I've got 'Plan A,' Corporal; rally the troops."

Seeing how I was the troops, I reported loud and clear, "Ready, Captain. All troops present and accounted for."

"Good. Excellent," Genie said as he leaped out of bed and into his clothes. He did this in one swift, fluid motion, and it was a sight to see. The moonlight was pouring through the bedroom window, making Genie look ten feet tall. "Attention! Listen up, troops, and listen good." Only the good Lord knew how much I hated to hear the words *listen up and listen good* because I knew the game was afoot and nothing or no one, save God, could stop it, and I was darn sure God had no intention of interfering. Anyway, He never had before, which led me to believe God was a bit of a gambler and liked to hang back and see how things turned out. I liked the idea of God being on Genie's side (our side), but being knee-deep in you-know-what, sitting in the dark on a tin tub with the devil himself beneath it, well, it gave me pause . . . and that's the truth.

At exactly 0600, my Captain appeared in the doorway of the chicken coop, fresh as a daisy. He smiled and handed me a steaming mug of chocolate and a bacon-and-egg sandwich. "I figured you could use this about now, Corporal Hall."

"Thank you, Sir. I sure am hungry, and boy, does this taste good." Genie watched me eat my sandwich and when the last bite went into my mouth, he shouted, and I jumped to attention.

"Forward, all you slip-slidin', hog-tyin', frog-fryin' sons-of-the-pioneers, march!" Genie loved making up his own military rallying songs for the troops. (Troops still meaning me, of course.) He never used the same one twice. Genie was truly one extraordinary kid. I often thought if someone was to open up Genie's head and look inside, he'd see nothing but a huge island of words, all kinds, foreign, too, and words not yet invented. Genie was a walking, talking book of knowledge.

"Corporal Hall?"

"Yes, Sir."

"Did you sleep well last night? Are you ready to carry out 'Plan A'?"

"Affirmative, Sir." *Affirmative* was a new word Genie had recently taught me. He liked to hear me use it. As for sleeping, I hadn't slept a wink. But early on in your military training, you learn your Captain does not, I repeat, *does not* want to hear about how well you slept or if you slept at all. Captains only want to hear, "Yes, Sir," and "Ready, Sir."

"Splendid, Corporal Hall. Where is the prisoner?"

"Under the tub, Sir, where we left him."

"Right. Okay, Corporal, you may bring him out."

"Out where, Sir?"

"Outside, of course, onto the Parade Ground where he is to be sentenced. The charges against him must be read aloud to everyone assembled." Another strange thing about being in an Army, or as it is in my case, being *the* Army, is you're not allowed to think for yourself but at the same time, you'd better be able to think quick on your feet.

I knew the parade ground had to be the barnyard, but I didn't have a clue as to whom or what might be assembled. This fact worried me more than a little bit. It was times like this when my Mom used to say, "Oh, just play one card and wish you'd played another, cause it don't matter." I guess it was fine for Mom, but it drove the rest of us crazy, especially when we had a big game of Pinochle going.

Once more, I tied the rope to my ankle and began dragging the tub along the same route we came in on. But it was tough going because Big Red and his lady friends were making a terrible ruckus, causing the old tin tub to literally dance around the slippery floor. The sounds coming from under the tub were definitely not the strains of the "Star Spangled Banner." Finally, I made it to the doorway of the chicken coop. The fresh air smelled heavenly.

"Halt! That's far enough, Corporal Hall."

"Right, Sir." I saluted my Captain. I then began to untie the rope around my ankle.

"Now, Corporal, I want you to pull the tub as close to the edge of the door step and just slightly over the stoop. When Big Red pokes his head out, and he will, I'll slip this noose around his neck and by all that's holy, we'll have him. Understood, Corporal?"

"Understood, Sir." Like everything else in my brief but turbulent life as a soldier, most everything was easier ordered than done. I knew this operation was no exception. As soon as the rays of sunlight lit up the inside of the tub, Big Red poked his neck out, right on cue. Genie did manage to slip the noose around his neck, but as he tried to pull it tight, Big Red dashed out from under the tub in a flash of feathers and angry squawks. Big Red hurdled himself to the ground, leaving his ladies to fend for themselves. Genie still had hold of the rope and was right behind him. Genie was desperately trying to reel Big Red in. Instead, the two of them were going around and around in a circle. It was Captain Ahab and Moby Dick; it was the Keystone Kops; it was Little Black Sambo and the tigers. It was pure mayhem, a pandemonium three-ring circus.

Casting off my entire military demeanor and risking tons of demerits, I fell to the ground, laughing in a fit of glorious glee. Every time Big Red and Genie whizzed by me, he would scream, "On your feet, Corporal, and can the laughter!" It took an enormous effort, but I finally pulled myself together and rose to my feet as Genie rushed by me in a blur. Big Red was hot on his heels. As they ran, the circle got smaller and smaller. It was hard to see who was chasing whom. Genie looked terrible, red-faced and exhausted, while Big Red looked like he could go another five miles. I stopped laughing and began to worry.

Genie yelled, "Corporal Hall, get the stake, get the stake! Put it here, right here!" He was pointing to the center of the barnyard, the Parade Ground. He kept shouting this order repeatedly. The stake Genie was screaming about was a four-foot pole. I knew exactly where it was and I raced to fetch it out of the barn. I retrieved the stake and ran as fast as I could to the center of the barnyard, dodging Genie and Big Red as I went. On the way, I grabbed a large stone to pound the stake into the ground. The moment I finished securing the stake, Genie and Big Red raced by me. However, this time Genie managed by some miracle to loop the rope around the stake. Big Red didn't notice his flight pattern was becoming smaller and tighter. Suddenly, to my never-ending relief, this well-oiled running machine found his fine-feathered self wrapped around the stake, tight as a drum. He screeched and wailed to a fare thee well, but his cries fell on deaf ears. Genie tied a big knot around Big Red's middle section while receiving several hard pecks on the top of his head.

Finally, Genie collapsed onto the grass, took a deep breath, and announced: "The prisoner is secured."

"That was mighty fine work, Captain, Sir," I said proudly, offering him my canteen of cold apple cider. Genie, with a grateful smile, proceeded to drink it down to the very last drop.

"Thanks, Corporal, I needed that."

"You're welcome, Sir." Meanwhile, the Parade Ground was filling up. Cows, chickens, Old Molly, Bruno (our lovable, ancient Blue Tick hound), Miss Lucy, Calico cat, and our little flock of Bantams had all wandered over to see what all the commotion was about.

Genie looked over at the assemblage and asked, "Where is Sergeant Spot?"

"Sir, Sergeant Spot is on rabbit duty."

"Very well, Corporal. We shall carry on without him." Despite his haggard body, Genie stood smartly at attention to address all those in attendance: "Attention all you bag of bones far from home, fearless drones, Kings of the Road. Listen up!" Genie's latest rally cry did not seem appropriate, but it was not for me to question my leader. As for the grand assembly, they couldn't care less. I was finding it hard to keep a straight face, myself. Reddy, my cow, spotted me and ambled over for a treat and a nudge, a love nudge.

Genie saw Reddy and commanded, "Clear your area, Corporal Hall. Smarten up!" I tried gently to push Reddy away from me, but she would have none of it. Instead, I stepped away from her, declaring that my area, my perimeter, had been cleared.

Genie marched to the center of the Parade Ground, as it were, to stand directly in front of Big Red, who had never stopped squawking or pecking at his ropes. Genie produced a white sheet of paper from his back pocket and began to read its contents with great authority: "Big Red, previously of Gooseneck Creek, Tennessee, you are hereby charged in the presence of God, the United States Indiana Farm Reserve Corps, and honored guests to hear the following crimes you have committed:

1. Assault and battery with intent to kill your employer, Clyde Nelson.
2. Six counts of out and out murder against your fellow creatures, including one Hampshire hog, pregnant at the time of the attack. One duck, name of Winnie, four baby kittens not yet named, Tommy the mole, Elsie, the oldest living laying hen in Grant County, three white barn owls, numerous rabbits, squirrels, birds, and six opossums.
3. Rape of several underage brown hens.
4. Assault and battery on Corporal Hall on three separate occasions, while she was standing guard duty.
5. Insubordination to the highest level.

Furthermore, you have steadfastly refused to alter, in any way, your criminal activities. You have shown no remorse. To the contrary, following each of these dastardly deeds, you have actually crowed about them: Do you have anything to say on your own behalf, before sentence is passed?" As it turns out, Big Red had plenty to say, all of which is unprintable! Big Red bellowed his endless obscenities, but Genie's booming voice drowned him out. "Big Red, you are hereby sentenced to death, to be carried out immediately on this 12th day of June 1943."

Earlier, Genie had told me the plan was to drown Big Red in the horse trough, then cook and eat him. It sounded like a great plan to me. "Corporal Hall?"

"Sir?"

"You may remove the stake from the ground and aid me in escorting the prisoner to the place of execution."

"Yes, Sir." I quickly did as I was ordered, remembering to keep my head low to avoid Big Red's sharp beak. My Captain and I proceeded to drag him over to the horse trough, which was up against the fence near the barn gate. By the time we got him there, most of the rope had come loose except from around his neck. With super-human strength, we managed to pull Big Red up and over the rim of the trough and into the water. The water in the trough measured about four-and-a-half feet deep.

As the noose slid off Big Red's neck, he sensed his impending doom. He began thrashing about wildly, slapping the water with his powerful wings and pecking at anything he could see, mainly Genie and me. Genie and I were soon bleeding from dozens of razor-sharp cuts; our hands were downright bloody. Genie was trying with all his strength to hold Big Red's head under water, but Big Red was clearly winning the battle.

"Corporal Hall!"

"Yes, Sir?"

"Jump in there, Corporal, and hold the prisoner down while I choke him."

"Are you crazy?" Once again, I had forgotten my military discipline.

"Get into the trough, Corporal, that's an order; get in now, JUMP!" I jumped and immediately felt the cold water rise to my chest. I grabbed for Big Red's wings and tried pushing them down next to his body. Failing at this, I then sat on him while Genie held his head under the water. Big Red put up one heck of a struggle, but at last, I felt his body go limp beneath me. "He's dead, Genie, I mean, Captain, Sir. The Big Red Monster is dead!" I was laughing and crying as I scrambled out of the tank, falling over the side to the ground next to my weary Captain.

"Damn good job, Corporal. You'll receive a medal for this detail. I repeat, well done, Corporal Hall." No sooner had those supreme words left Genie's mouth when suddenly all hell broke loose. Big Red was far from being dead. He came splashing, screeching, and careening over the top of the horse trough like the evil fiend he was, scratching and pecking, his wings cutting us to pieces. He was in our faces; my cheeks ran red with blood, and Genie's arm had been slit open from shoulder to wrist. We stood up to run. Big Red was staggering, flapping his wings, and making horrible noises. The beast had murder in his eyes, and he was running straight at us.

"Oh my, God! Genie, Big Red is going to kill us." I was so scared I had wet my pants.

"Not if we can get him first, Janny. Pull yourself together, Corporal Hall. This is war, and you and I are in it up to our lilywhite necks! Follow me!" At this point, I watched as my Captain became a wild man. He chased Big Red around the barnyard like a man possessed. I decided to follow suit. When Big Red, still a touch waterlogged, stumbled and fell to the ground, we were on him like bees to a honeycomb. We beat him senseless with our bare fists. I got in a couple of good licks with a rock. At last, Genie was able to grab the animal's feet and tie them together with the rope. Big Red was still full of fight, sputtering and pecking holes into our hands, which were beginning to look like raw meat; regardless of how we were hurting, we were determined to get the job done. We managed to drag Big Red through the barnyard gate and into the backyard, where we spread him out over a large flat stump Grandpa used as a chopping block. At the stump, it was Dante's Inferno. It was kill or be killed.

I could only hold one wing down at a time because Big Red's wingspan was longer than my arms could reach. But none of this mattered. Genie and I had but one thought: it was him or us. "Big Red is going down, Janny. He's going down." That phrase became our fight song, and we sang out loud and clear. Genie grabbed hold of Grandpa's red-handled axe, leaned forward against the stump, and gave Big Red a mighty whack, missing his neck completely and chopping off half of his razor-sharp beak instead. "Now, you red devil, try and bite us!"

No sooner had those words left Genie's mouth than Big Red lunged up into Genie's face, ripping out a big chunk of his cheek. The impact of such horrible pain caused Genie to stumble backwards a couple of steps. One thing became crystal clear: half a beak or no beak,

Big Red was a killer who was prepared to fight to the death, be it his or ours. With blood gushing from the hole in his cheek, Genie screamed in pain, "Hold him, Janny! Hold him!" I don't know how, but I held him down. I think I threw my body across his chest. I was crying (very unbecoming to a soldier), but things were getting mighty scary.

"Stop crying, Corporal Hall! We are in the throes of battle; slide off his chest and try to grab the underside of his wings," Genie's strong voice gave me courage. I got a good hold beneath Big Red's wings then leaned backwards as far as I could and still keep hold of him. In the next instant, Genie delivered a powerful blow that lopped off Big Red's left wing. Feathers, blood, and hide were coming at me from every direction. "Keep your mouth closed, Corporal Hall." He didn't have to tell me twice; I gladly obeyed. Big Red began slapping me hard with his remaining good wing. I gritted my teeth and bit my lip. I looked across at Genie; his face had turned to stone. His eyes were calm and fixed on his objective: Big Red's neck. My Captain reared back and swung the axe with colossal force. The axe came down clean, hard, and fast, severing Big Red's head from his body. His head sailed into the air like a rocket to the moon. Genie and I watched it go. We were speechless and covered from head to toe in blood, gore, and feathers. We were a bloody sight, but by Heaven, we were victorious!

We danced around the stump singing the Notre Dame Fight Song. We weren't Catholic, but Genie said Notre Dame had one hell of a great fight song. As we were celebrating, we suddenly noticed to our horror Big Red's headless body had not yet given up the ghost. To our dismay, the body was running around in circles actually passing by us. I was so exhausted I fell to the ground. Genie had witnessed my fall and shouted at me, "On your feet, Corporal Hall. As long as that headless bastard is still standing, we will do likewise." I got to my feet feeling terribly shaky, but thank God, in another few minutes, Big Red's body finally keeled over. Genie and I were quick to follow. Not able to speak, Genie grabbed hold of my hand and squeezed once. I squeezed back twice. The psycho known as Big Red was dead. We had saved everyone, man and beast. Genie was well pleased and announced justice had been done. Then he stood up, looked out over the corn fields and shouted, "Bring on those Nazi rats: we're ready for them!"

Grandma, who had watched the final minutes of this historic battle from behind the kitchen's screened door, worried out loud as to what damage may have been perpetuated onto our character. Grandpa arrived later in the evening and unlike Grandma, he was enormously pleased with his brave grandchildren. He could readily see that we were the walking wounded, and he took great care tending our cuts, bruises, and minor injuries. He used up the Clover Salve, two bottles of Mercurochrome, and naturally a bottle of Vick's, which was used to cure everything, no matter what.

There was much applause and singing when Grandma shoved Big Red's carcass into her black cast iron oven. Grandma made cornbread stuffing, mashed potatoes, giblet gravy, and fresh string beans, accompanied by light-as-a-cloud golden biscuits with my fresh churned butter and wild strawberry jam. Topping the dinner off was apple cobbler and butterscotch pie. It was a meal fit for a king and queen—exactly what Genie and I felt like. Big Red came out of the oven a rich golden brown, and he smelled delicious. Grandma asked me to say the blessing, and I said the only short one I knew from our father's side of the family: "Our Heavenly Father, look down upon us and pardon our many sins. Thank you for these table blessings, in Jesus' name, Amen."

In honor of Genie, Grandpa carved him the first slice. Genie was beaming as he took his first bite. All at once, a look of sheer horror came over his face. You guessed it; Big Red had the last laugh: he was too tough to eat. Neither Spot nor Bruno could swallow a single hunk of the old monster's hide. Spot carried his piece outside and buried it for another day. Bruno left his on the floor with a look of deprivation in his big brown eyes, as if he had been mistreated. Seeing his confusion, Grandma gave him a plate of stuffing and gravy, which he devoured instantly, wagging his tail in appreciation. Spot chose to go rabbit hunting.

So, there we sat, all in our places with sun-shiny faces, not able to eat our grand celebration dinner. Suddenly, Grandpa began to laugh. His big loud wonderful laugh filled up the whole house. Then we all started to laugh and couldn't stop. I was holding my stomach, and Genie was slapping his knees.

"Well, Sir, I'll be damned," Grandpa said his eyes twinkling.

"Well, Sir, I'll be damned," Genie said, his eyes shining like two pewter dollars in a mud hole. Nobody corrected Genie's language, not on this occasion. Crazy with laughter, Genie began to give Grandpa a blow-by-blow description of the capture, the fight of the century, the victory, and execution of the vicious, bloodthirsty, heartless, villain Big Red.

"Worst damn trade I ever made." Each time Grandpa repeated this phrase, Genie and I fell off our chairs in uncontrollable glee.

Grandma came out of the kitchen with a platter of smoked ham. Farmers always have an extra ham in the pantry, and it tasted great. After we ate and laughed some more, Grandma said, "Before you and your partner in crime head off for bed, I want you to bury your kill. Bury it in the cherry orchard, and bury it deep." Genie and I never questioned Grandma, not that we couldn't, for she was not like our father, who believed children should never question adults. Rather, it was simply out of respect for a great lady. We both said "Okay," but I caught a funny look in Genie's eyes, which meant something was up.

While I washed up the dishes, Genie read Emerson to Grandma. After our grandparents went to bed, Genie wrapped Big Red's body in a clean flour sack. We went outside and walked slowly towards the cherry orchard. As we passed by the stump where Big Red had met his Waterloo, we noted Grandma had scrubbed it clean and hosed down the ground around it. There was not a trace of blood, feathers, or gore, nothing to suggest the carnage that had taken place a few hours ago.

Genie was quiet as we walked along, but I know something was spinning 'round in his mind. I also knew he would tell me soon. At the gate leading into the cherry orchard, Genie said solemnly, "Janny, I'm not going to do it. I'm not giving this monster a decent burial. He doesn't deserve it, and we both know it."

"You're right, Genie, I hate the idea of his remains resting next to Molly Kitten, who he murdered in cold blood!"

"Exactly. That's my point."

"Well, what are you going to do with him?"

I knew Genie had already thought of something, as he always had a "Plan A" and a "Plan B" ready. Genie was in charge, strong, and confident.

"I'll tell you what we're going to do, Corporal Hall. We're going to burn the S.O.B. at the stake!"

"Genie, it's a great plan; it's perfect: it's retribution," I said proudly.

"Hey, another new word?"

"Yes, I learned it in Grandma's Sunday School class."

"I'm proud of you, Corporal, very proud. Now, I want you to get some straw and kindling wood, and I'll fetch the stake."

We went about our tasks posthaste. Genie was whistling a Johnny Mercer tune. He made the fire and when it was extremely hot with red sparks flying up into the night sky, Genie bound Big Red's headless, golden carcass to the stake and placed it in the middle of the fire.

We sat on the ground, our eyes transfixed, watching in silence as Big Red turned first to red, then black, and finally to a heap of white ash. A couple of his bones didn't burn up; Genie said they were his tough old leg bones. It was a curious sight, all right, but for me, a satisfying one. I don't know for sure how Genie felt. When the last ember died away, Genie said, almost whispering, "There's a lesson to be learned here, Janny. I mean, Corporal Hall."

I didn't like the tone of Genie's voice, as I was very familiar with this particular tone. To my mind, my beloved brother had but one major flaw: he was forever and ever hell-bent on "lessons to be learned." He could drive a whole Marine platoon crazy, meaning me, of course, with his "lessons to be learned" routine. As for me, I could have happily gotten by with much less education on these matters. But Genie was older, my mentor, my best friend, and my Captain, and he did know everything about everything. That much was a given.

Finally, offering my best "okay" smile, I asked, "Genie, are you saying you're sorry about killing Big Red, that we did something wrong?"

"No, I'm not saying I'm sorry. Big Red deserved exactly what he got. Besides, Grandpa asked me to get rid of him, and I did. *We* did."

"Well, Sir . . .Captain, Sir, I'm not sure I understand what you are talking about, but it was plain to me Big Red was out to kill us. It was him or us. Remember, he was found guilty fair and square. To my way of thinking, we are heroes."

"You're absolutely correct, Corporal Hall. It was a search and destroy mission, pure, if not so simple."

I could tell my Captain was getting back on track until he began speaking in long sentences, something about our enjoying it so much.

"Yes, Corporal Hall, I think I know the lesson here to be learned . . ."

Honestly, I didn't hear another word. I was falling asleep. I knew I loved and admired my brother. I understood he was the kind of person who had to cover all the bases, figure all the angles, tie up any loose ends, and above all, do the right thing whenever possible. I had long ago accepted this quirk in an otherwise sterling character.

This had been a truly unforgettable day in the history of my young life. Genie had proven himself a great leader on the field of battle. Big Red may have been a rooster, renown among his species, but he was Nazi through and through. Genie had been fearless, and I'd done my part, too. I felt good!

One thing was for certain, if those Nazis did attack our farm, they would be forever sorry they met up with Captain Dewey Eugene Hall. Big Red was only the beginning. This was war!

Chapter Two:

Dewey Eugene Hall

Having killed Big Red, the odious, ogre of Murder Incorporated, I am now free to begin our story.

In Chapter One, you met the inexplicable and inexhaustible Captain Dewey Eugene Hall, known affectionately to me as Genie. Genie was the major influence in my life, bar none. It was Genie who shaped my character and did his level best to give me a sense of hope, home, and honor. Genie always took the high ground and tried to teach me to do the same. Most of our adventures took place on those shabby 40 acres of heaven.

Genie was a remarkable lad on many levels. At a very young age, he took me to raise. He did so with unconditional love, without keeping track of the cost to himself or worrying about the why.

He took me by the hand with laughter in his eyes and love in his heart, to play amongst the stars and sail the seas of imagination for as long as time would allow.

Dewey Eugene Hall was the kind of kid parents dreamed about: smart, good-looking, articulate, curious, funny, 99% honest, and he could get along with anybody. He was tall with a quickness to his step. He had things to do and places to go, a wealth of jet-black hair and eyes to match. He had neither an arrogant bone in his body, nor was he conceited. Genie honestly believed, without a doubt, the world was his oyster and opportunity was about to knock on his door. He was ready, willing, and able to take charge. As it turned out, the first thing Genie was asked to take charge of was me.

It began the day I was born, April 28, 1936, on a cool, rainy spring morning in the tiny community of Jonesboro, Indiana. I made my debut atop a white metal kitchen table above a men's barbershop. In attendance for this less then momentous occasion were a mid-wife, the barber, two customers, and Genie. Not expected for several weeks, I arrived nevertheless, six pounds and yellow as a crooked neck squash, totally jaundiced. Like my brother, I was crowned with masses of blue-black hair in ringlets flowing down my back in thick, uneven waves.

I must have been quite a sight. The mid-wife announced, "She's a right pretty lil' thing Miz Hall but yellow as a ripe pear. And Lord knows we gotta do somethin' about all that hair." Having made her announcement, she motioned to the barber to come cut my hair. As he was removing the thick black hair, she took her scissors and cut the umbilical cord that bound me to my extremely ill mother.

Our mother had suffered numerous miscarriages and the loss of my sister, Mary Anna Ella, who had lived for five precious days. The mid-wife predicted I would not live past three.

Grandma Nelson arrived and proceeded to prove the prediction wrong. She began by emptying out the largest drawer in a huge old bureau. She lined it with hot water bottles, blankets, and set it in front of our pot-bellied stove. Genie provided one of his flannel shirts to serve as my bunting, and then Grandma laid me gently down into my own little pine-scented crib. To this day, I love the smell of pine. Meanwhile, the men from the barbershop went out and brought back a case of Carnation milk. Someone stretched a black nipple, used for feeding baby calves, over a nickel Coca-Cola bottle, and I was in business.

Genie had been present for the birth of Mary Anna Ella, and he was present when she died and was buried. When I was older, he told me about her funeral. He said she looked like a baby doll, except she didn't have any eyebrows or eyelashes. When he held her tiny hands in his, he saw she didn't have fingernails. He said Grandma Nelson gathered purple lilacs from the back yard and tucked them in around Mary Anna Ella's body, and he helped. Her casket was not even as big as his red wagon, but it was pretty, pure white with a wooden cross carved on the top. A man handed our father a perfect pink rose from his yard. He laid it across the casket. No one gave Genie a flower, so he reached inside his back pocket and took out his lucky rabbit's foot. He then stepped up to the casket and placed his rabbit's foot next to the rose. Genie said he felt our father's hand on his head.

Then folks bowed their heads and someone said a prayer. During the prayer, Genie looked up and saw our mother looking down on him from her bedroom window. He said he would never forget how sad she looked and he would remember for always the sweet scent of lilacs.

In the days that followed, mother never spoke about Mary Anna Ella, but she would tell everyone God had sent me to replace her. I never understood what being sent by God really meant, but it worried me.

Genie told me not to worry because there were a whole bunch of things said and unsaid between grownups and children which are never explained so you can understand. He told me grownups were terribly busy people and I should come and ask him my questions, so I did.

Grandparents, on the other hand, are different. They always have time for you. Grandpa would stop in the middle of a row he was plowing to listen to Genie. And Grandma would stop whatever she was doing, wipe her hands on her apron, and look you straight in the eye and say, "Now, child, what's troubling you so?"

Genie and I both knew our Grandma Nelson was an angel living as our Grandmother here on earth. She would take me on nature walks into the woods. She knew every plant, wildflower, tree, and bird. She had been a teacher in a one-room schoolhouse, a red one of course. She was always teaching, but in such a loving way you didn't mind. I never knew what we might discover or what she would ask me. One time, she said, "Janny, girl, which is more important to you, learning exactly how a bird flies or simply enjoying the fact the bird flies?"

The question seemed hard at first but as we walked and watched birds flying overhead, I knew my answer. I enjoyed seeing them fly because they took me with them. I was hesitant about my answer but spoke it truly.

Grandma put her arms around me and said, "You'll not grow up to be a scientist, Janny: you'll be a writer and a poet."

Imagine how much I loved her for knowing my heart's desire when I hadn't told a single soul, not even Genie, but she knew. Grandparents are made special so they can see inside a child's heart.

Genie and I were lucky to have such grandparents. My father had adored his mother, whose name was Ella, but she died before I was born, after birthing 15 children. Daddy named me Janet Louella so I had her name, but I was never called Janet Louella. I was called Janny from the beginning. Dewey Eugene was called Genie, so now we were Genie and Janny. The names fit and have stood the test of time. To this day, we are Genie and Janny.

The Great Depression was supposed to be nearly over by the time I came along, but such was not the case with us. The Depression had settled down around people's shoulders; they walked bent over from carrying this heavy burden. Mom often said, "Keeping body and soul together was a 24-hour job and folks' troubles were as unrelenting as raindrops on a drowning man." It wasn't the best of times for another child to be born into the Hall family.

Sadly for us, our mother remained confined to her bed. She said little, smoked a lot, and rarely laughed. The only talk in our house was about the Depression. They talked about it day in and day out. Genie told me he thought grownups were strange. He said they talked about hard times as if they were the only ones affected. Naturally, kids didn't talk about hard times as such, but we knew all about hard times in a most poignant way. Genie said kids suffered too, but didn't have any way to deal with it. Crisis in our house came as regular as the milkman. I had lots of fears and Genie had what he called "the dreads." These things went unnoticed by our over-worked parents. I was glad I had Genie, but he had no one.

Before continuing about my brother, I want to tell you a little more about our father. Our father was the seventh son of a seventh son, so he had seven names: Commer Dore Dewey Curtis Jackson Manning Hall. To his folks, he was known as Dink. At his job, he was C.D. Hall. Mom called him Dewey. He was 5'11" tall with hazel eyes and beautiful black, wavy hair. He was thin as a rail and tough as nails. He spoke with a slow, rich, creamy southern drawl; he was a true Georgia cracker. He stuttered badly when he got upset. Indiana Hoosiers had a devil of a time trying to understand him. When he did land a job, he'd lose it because if he thought someone was making fun of his speech, he'd jump on them, give them a good thrashing, and was fired.

Grandma Nelson was soft-spoken and possessed keen insights and depths of ingenuity that belied even her Angel status. She understood our father and quietly set about helping him to overcome his stuttering. She soon realized he needed other help, as well. In Georgia, he had completed the sixth grade. He did not do well in school because he was forever fighting. He was a fighting machine who never knew when to quit. The principal, Mr. Morgan G. Morgan, happened to be dating one of Daddy's pretty sisters at the time, but that fact didn't help matters. Daddy was expelled at the ripe age of eleven. He never set foot in a schoolroom again, which included every school Genie and I attended. From that time forward, pride became our father's ultimate deceiver, his mask, and finally, his heartrending executioner.

There was about Daddy a kind of rogue mystic, a swagger, and a sense of danger. He was a man's man, but women openly flirted with him. Genie told me Daddy was a hard worker, a decent guy who longed to be anything other than what he was. Genie said Daddy really wanted to be a boxer (no surprise there), and he didn't mind being a bit shady now and again. In his youth, he played a little trumpet in New Orleans. Whenever he could, he played jazz at funerals and was paid a buck fifty out and a buck and a quarter on the way back. Otherwise, he played in the French Quarter for his supper, drinks, and cigarettes. He was too young for any of it, but nobody asked questions in New Orleans.

Around 1939, he was in New Orleans with a buddy and they went to hear the great tenor saxophonist Coleman Hawkins. Daddy said when he played "Body and Soul," there wasn't a dry eye in the club, including the men.

Throughout our life, Daddy had buddies who would appear out of the blue and they'd take off together for several days at a time. Mom never said how she felt about this. She accepted the fact that these men were important to Daddy, some he had grown up with and ran whiskey for when times were tough.

At one point in time during the Depression, Daddy moved us to Florida with his kinfolk. He worked running whiskey for the family, until the revenuers found the still. Daddy's brother-in-law, Stan, was sent to Raiford for seven years of hard labor. Stan never gave up Daddy or any of the others. Daddy then took us back to Indiana. Stan did his time, got out, and continued in the whiskey-making business. Stan was married to Daddy's favorite sister, Velma. They looked so much alike as to pass for twins. One night, Stan was coming home late when his brand new Packard stalled on the tracks at a rail crossing. The train hit the Packard doing 80 miles an hour. Daddy said, by all counts, Stan was one hell of a good guy and didn't deserve such a bad ending. Velma went a little crazy over Stan's death and started drinking. On and off when she was down and out, she called from Chattahoochee, the state mental hospital in North Florida. She was crying and asking for cigarettes and money. Genie told me Daddy sent both. He never heard from her again. She adored Genie and she called me "pretty baby." Genie and I loved her, too. Even with the drinking and getting older, Velma was an enthrallingly beautiful woman.

Back in Indiana, Daddy and Grandpa worked at whatever jobs they could find. Whoever worked brought home the food, and our family ate a whole lot: fried fish, fried chicken, fried rabbit, fried squirrel, fried potatoes, fried eggs, fried mush, and stewed possum. Sweet tea was served winter and summer, and the table was never without biscuits and sugar cane syrup for us and sorghum for Daddy.

I loved my father from a distance. I was in awe of him and a little afraid of him, as he had a terrible temper. Genie was my father and in truth my mother, too.

On day five of my life, my father took Genie out onto the tiny back porch to ask him what he thought of his new baby sister. Grandma was there, too, and said Genie did not hesitate in answering Daddy's question. "She's awfully small, don't cry much, and she's the prettiest thing I ever saw."

Daddy placed his hands on Genie's thin shoulders and said, "Genie, you know your Grandpa and I have to go anywhere we can to find work. No doubt, we'll be riding the rails. Your Mom can't get out of bed and your Grandma is holding down two jobs."

Grandma related later how Genie stood there straight as an arrow, his eyes never leaving our father's face. Grandma said our father's voice sounded serious and sad. "Son, you are going to have to grow up pretty doggone fast. You're going to be the man of the house, and most important of all, you will be in charge of your baby sister. You must feed her, dress her, and watch to see no harm comes to her of any kind. We don't want any more funerals around here, now do we?"

"No, Sir, we don't want any more funerals 'round here."

"Can you handle this, son? Can you be my little man?"

"Yes, Sir, Daddy, I can be your little man. I'll take real good care of Janny. I won't let anything bad happen to her, and I'll help Mommy get well."

"You're a good boy, a fine little man, Genie. I'm very proud of you and so are Grandma and Grandpa."

Like I said, this kid was every parent's dream. Dewey Eugene Hall was seven-years-old going on 40. Genie took me on as his prime mission in life. After all, I was better than a puppy: I could walk, talk, obey, and love him unconditionally, and I did.

Mom finally got better and went to work in a factory. Babysitters came and went, but mostly it was Genie and me.

Genie was my universe: I adored him. He taught me to play patty-cake, peek-a-boo, and here's the church, here's the steeple, open the door, and see all the people. He showed me how to button my buttons, tie my shoes, brush my teeth, hold a kitten, pet a dog, throw a ball, climb trees, ride a broomstick pony, and fly the kites he made himself out of thin wood from orange crates, newspaper, and scraps of bright cloth from Grandma's sewing basket. He taught me to talk in sentences, swim, swing from a rope, dig holes for forts, pound a nail, tell a story, keep a secret, color in the lines, and memorize poems. He taught me to play marbles, and he taught me Morse code. He gave me stacks of books to read and afterwards, he'd ask me questions on what I'd read. The one thing I could never learn was to whistle. Genie was a great whistler. He never gave up on me, but I never did learn to whistle. He also made me memorize every song Johnny Mercer ever wrote.

At the time of my birth, Jonesboro had a population of less than 100 people. Everybody in town knew Genie; they called him "The Little Man." Every afternoon, Genie took me for a walk. Our first stop was a visit with Mr. and Mrs. Rice, an elderly couple who lived four doors down from the barbershop and our apartment. They enjoyed sitting on their porch and sipping homemade beer.

Mr. Rice had been a seafaring man, having joined the Navy when he was seventeen. He had sailed around the world and loved telling us stories about his adventures. Somewhere in his travels, he had acquired Tom. Tom was a bright green Macaw, a fine-looking parrot and the first parrot Genie and I had ever seen.

Mr. Rice said Tom came from one of the small islands in the Pacific, but he could never remember which one. He said all those islands looked alike to him, kind of like big cupcakes floating in a row. Mrs. Rice told us that one day, while Mr. Rice's ship was docked taking on supplies, the parrot flew on board landing on Seaman Rice's shoulder and refused to leave.

When Seaman Rice asked the parrot his name, the parrot replied, squawking clearly, "My name is Tom. My name is Tom."

However, following this exchange, the parrot never again answered to the name Tom. He would only answer to the name Polly. Genie said parrots were a strange lot, bordering on weird.

Genie would walk up to Tom and say, "Polly want a cracker?"

Tom/Polly would cock his shiny green head at Genie, look him straight in the eye and scream, "HELL NO! Polly wants cake!"

No matter how many times this scene was repeated, Genie and I would laugh ourselves silly. As for Tom/Polly, he never ate a bite of cake in his life; he only ate crackers.

Our second stop was the bakery owned by Mr. and Mrs. Huff. The Huffs were as round as their doughnuts and every bit as sweet. They gave us short bread cookies with pink icing and glasses of cold milk. "For your journey," Mrs. Huff would say, smoothing her apron and smiling her special smile. They had no children of their own and had become very fond of us.

Mr. Huff loved Genie and enjoyed watching him collect, repair, and sell toy cars. Besides knowing everything about everything, Genie was blessed with the gift of gab; he was a born salesman. The gift of gab came from whom else, Grandpa Nelson, Grant County's best talker and superior horse trader.

Grandpa Nelson was a gentle and beguiling huckster. What set him apart from being a plain ordinary crook was the fact he genuinely loved people and wouldn't cheat anybody out of anything. It was the "game" he adored, pure and simple flim-flam. He was in his glory buying, selling, and closing a hard won deal. He took Genie to auctions and other places so he could learn first-hand how deals were made. Genie, being a quick study, soon became a junior spieler of some renown in this small oasis of Jonesboro, Indiana. Genie proved to be an apt apprentice, honing his skills rapidly. In no time at all, Genie had a whole fleet of toy cars all in mint condition. He carried them in a special Cuban cigar box he found in an empty railroad boxcar.

Genie had deals working up and down Main Street. He would even go so far as repossessing a car if a deal went sour, or the new owner failed to keep the car in good shape.

For a dime down and a nickel a week, you could have the car of your dreams. The old men loved it; it was the best game in town. I don't think the old men knew how serious "the game" was to Genie, but I knew. We were close and knew in our hearts what the other was feeling. Genie was not a complainer, but he didn't mind when I complained. He'd listen and then explain to me just how this old world worked.

As for me, I complained when I fell down, when I got scared, or wanted attention. Genie was there to make everything right again. Genie was truly the man of the house, and he took his responsibility to me seriously.

The monies he earned from selling his cars he gave to Mom. A handful of nickels and dimes would easily buy bread and milk. After a year or so, Genie had sold or traded all of his cars except a little blue roadster, a nifty gal with real rubber tires, a sleek steel chassis, and a rumble seat that actually opened up. I knew Genie loved that car; it was his favorite. I knew he wanted to keep it for himself, but when Mr. Huff offered him $5 for it, Genie couldn't turn down such a large sum of money. He accepted the offer and delivered the car himself, parking it in the window of Mr. Huff's bakery. Everyone who passed by admired it and most of the passers-by knew who had owned it.

The little roadster's sky-blue paint never faded, though it sat in the direct sunlight for 40 years until Mr. Huff died. After Mr. Huff's passing, the building was torn down. The blue roadster was not found among the debris.

If by chance, grownups should ever tell you a child of three or four is too young to remember things they have experienced, don't believe them! I remember Tom the parrot, Mr. and Mrs. Rice, cookies with pink icing, cold milk served with warm hugs and the glorious taste of black walnut ice cream cones on a hot summer's day. I also remember how Genie cried silent tears when he parked the little blue roadster in Mr. Huff's window. I remember because it was the first time I had seen my brother cry.

In spite of hard times, babies dying, and people you love having to be away from home, Genie said, "Remember, there's always tomorrow."

Genie was big on tomorrows. He often told me there were no free rides, which confused me, since he was always giving me free rides.

All I knew and cared about was being with Genie because it really was a grand one-of-a-kind ride. A ride Genie and I believed would never end.

Chapter Three:
Hard Times

Not long after Genie's "final deal" with his little blue roadster, our family left Jonesboro to live with our Grandparents. Hard times didn't follow us because hard times had never left.

Grandpa said, "Hard times is nothing but life trying to right itself after a bad fall."

Grandma said, "Hard times came because men were always digging holes for themselves when they ought to be out there moving mountains."

Grandpa's reply was, "I don't understand you, Florrie. I was paid a fair wage for every hole I ever dug."

There aren't any mountains in Indiana, but folks talked a lot about them: don't make a mountain out of a molehill; it takes faith to move a mountain; the bear went over the mountain to see what he could see, and Mom always had mountains of clothes to wash.

The only mountain I knew was the song Genie taught me: "Oh the buzzin' of the bees, in the cigarette trees / near the soda water fountain, at the lemonade springs / where the bluebird sings on the big rock candy mountain."

Hard times and mountains to climb about summed up our daily lives. People came and went to their jobs at all hours of the day and night. Grandma told us we all had a job to do no matter how small it was because it helped to keep the wheel turning.

We heard about folks losing their homes and not being able to feed their families. Genie told me before I was born, Mom and Dad had owned, rather they were paying on, a small farm. When the Depression hit, they lost it for lack of $60 and change. Mom was devastated, and Dad became bitter and enraged, so much so he vowed never again to own a piece of property, and he didn't until he retired some 40 years later.

While we had been living with our Grandparents, Grandma had not only managed to cure Dad of his stuttering but she had also guided him through Radio Correspondence School where he earned his diploma. She told Genie our father was a very smart man.

As a direct result of his accomplishment, Farnsworth who, at the time, manufactured Capehart Radios hired Daddy. Daddy was a natural when it came to understanding and fixing radios, and he loved his job.

Later, when Farnsworth was bought out by the giant R.C.A., Daddy lost his job. R.C.A. refused to hire him because he was blind in one eye, due to having yellow fever as a child. However, his other eye had double strength. Desperate, Daddy went to see his former boss at Farnsworth, who had retired, and told him that R.C.A. had refused to hire him. The very next day, Daddy received a call from R.C.A. telling him to come to work.

Daddy worked for R.C.A. until he retired. He was the highest paid blue-collar worker they had. Nobody knew more about those giant electronic machines than Daddy. Some of these energy producers were as big as a small house. When the company started making television sets, Daddy picked right up on this new invention and soon became an expert. Genie said Daddy had been asked to step up and take a boss's job, but turned it down every time. The other bosses had college degrees, and Daddy's pride would not allow him this added success.

After Daddy was hired by R.C.A., we moved to Marion, Indiana, which was about eight miles from Jonesboro, where I was born. The house we rented was pretty shabby; truth be told, it was down right revolting. One of our favorite radio programs was called "The Life of Riley." Riley, the main character, was blue-collar, like us. His favorite saying was "What a revoltin' development this is!" This pretty much summed up the house.

Despite Daddy's new job and our move to our own place, hard times continued. "Hard Times" became the fabric of our everyday speech. Folks would announce, "You may as well walk these Hard Times, cause you sure ain't gonna git no ride." These pearls of wisdom were accompanied by, "That's the God's truth if I ever heard it." And believe me, we heard it repeatedly.

As time went on, Genie and I were given more and more responsibility regarding the running of the house. I learned to iron everyone's clothes, which included starching and pressing my Dad's white shirts. Argo became my friend; Argo Starch and Duz does everything. What a pair! I had been ironing handkerchiefs and pillowcases for quite a long time. I liked it, in fact. But this new job was altogether overwhelming. Nevertheless, I became the perfect ironer at the age of eight. I was a real Mrs. Tiggywinkle.

I could cook, too. By age 12, I could prepare a complete turkey dinner with sage and onion stuffing, mashed potatoes and gravy, giblet gravy, fresh green beans, deviled eggs, pumpkin pie, and homemade biscuits.

Genie cooked as well. He was our expert short-order cook. He could fry a dozen eggs at one time in Mom's giant cast iron skillet. Sunny-side up, over easy, soft scrambled, or my personal favorite, fried flat as a pancake (which came out perfect every time).

Later, Genie became a short order cook to help pay his way through college. He graduated from Ball State College in 1954 in Muncie, Indiana. At home, we both had lots of chores and Genie was good to help. He would wash dishes, but never a pot, pan, or skillet. He argued that pots, pans, and skillets were not dishes and therefore, not part of the deal. However, possessing a great since of fair play, he would stay in the kitchen while I washed them up and put them away. He'd whistle Johnny Mercer tunes and I'd sing along. I didn't really mind doing the pots and pans because Genie made everything fun.

Genie simply loved the taste of whole white milk. He was forever in trouble about his drinking all the milk and putting the empty bottle back into the refrigerator. There was never money to buy extra milk, and chocolate milk was out of the question. Chocolate milk was the only milk I liked. From time to time, I'd wake to find a cold pint of chocolate milk next to my cheek on the pillow. I knew Genie had put it there and I never asked him how or where he got it. I made sure to put the empty bottle back under my pillow. I knew it would be gone the next day.

Genie loved impossible tasks, and he loved to argue. Arguing was his best suit. He could argue and charm you at the same time, which thoroughly confused his opponent. To my knowledge, Mom never won an argument with Genie. He'd wear her down to mush and she'd throw up her hands and declare, "Gene Hall, some things just aren't worth arguing about." Genie would flash his "I gottcha" smile, and Mom would laugh in spite of herself. Genie loved seeing Mom laugh, and he never missed an opportunity to make it happen.

Mom had a little saying for every occasion, situation, or problem that came our way. Genie took these in stride, but they drove me crazy. Growing up for me was one big obscure array of creeds, doctrines, rules, principles, theories, and plain old forbearance. Somewhere along the line, our mother and the *Readers' Digest* had formed an unshakable alliance. She decided there was enough wisdom between its covers (along with her Bible) to arm herself to do battle with every fear and foe, real or imagined. She couldn't have been more wrong, but one thing's for sure: she wasn't about to argue about it.

Mom suffered terribly with sinus headaches, but she'd go to work anyway. Having quit school in the seventh grade to marry our father, her job skills were limited. She worked at a shoe factory, a box factory, a paper factory, a radio factory, and one of her later jobs was with a laundry. Often, she would arrive home from the laundry, walk through the door, and fall over in a dead faint that lasted three or four minutes. It was my job to rouse her with chunks of ice rolled in a towel, some iced tea, and a piece of cold fried chicken. It was scary, but we got used to it. It was how we lived. Genie didn't say much during these episodes, but I could tell it bothered him. I took my cue from him. When all these worries gathered in our hearts, Genie called them heartaches, and he was right.

In spite of our help, it was plain to see Mom couldn't keep up her grueling pace. She quit her job at the laundry and the radio factory, and got a job at Hill's Department Store selling ladies' dresses.

Like her dad, Clyde Guy Nelson, Mom never met a stranger she couldn't talk to; Mom had found her niche. She was in her element, and she enjoyed the whole process. She earned something called PMs, which meant she got $0.50 extra on certain dresses and $0.75 on coats. Mom outsold everybody and had customers who refused to have anyone else wait on them.

One day after school, Genie and I had come uptown to the store with a message from Daddy. Mom was busy; she had three dressing rooms going at once. Genie watched, fascinated, and finally said, "Janny, our mom's a star!"

The Store Manager, Mr. Mott, whose family owned the store, knew he had found a gem in Mom. She dressed his wife and daughters and all his female relatives. Mr. Mott thought a great deal of Mom. As a favor to her, he allowed me to come work in the basement selling notions, going for coffee, Cokes, and doughnuts. Of course, my name did not appear on any payroll check and I didn't punch a time clock. I was paid in cash at the end of every week. I gave my pay envelope to my mother, and never once looked inside. I had not yet celebrated my fourteenth birthday.

Inventory time was the worst. Everyone stayed late, usually until 2 a.m. or later, and no one got paid, but Mr. Mott would open up the Coke machine, and we were allowed to drink all the Coca-Cola we could hold. Mr. Mott would send out for hamburgers and fries from The Grand Hamburg, which was right around the corner, and it was all free.

To earn more money, Daddy fixed people's radios on the side. One time, instead of money, a lady offered to give Genie and me piano lessons. Daddy loved music, especially piano music. He would listen to Frankie Carle and Carmen Cavello for hours. We had a huge, upright, solid black Baldwin that weighed a ton and took up one whole wall of the living room.

Mom could play by ear, and her favorite piece was "Long Ago and Far Away," usually followed by "My Darlin,' Clementine . . . .wearing boxes without top-ses, and her shoes were #9." Genie was less than happy and never spent much time practicing, but I loved learning the piano and was soon playing out of a book titled *Easy Piano Classics*. When I learned to play "Stardust" and the old hymn "He'll Understand and Say Well Done," it was the first time I felt my Daddy was proud of me. He'd have me play them repeatedly; he never tired of hearing them. Genie and I played "Chopsticks" and "Boogie Woogie"; we were good! We did one number together which brought the house down every time. We played and sang "A Shanty in Old Shantytown." We'd have the old Baldwin quakin' and movin' on across the floor. It was such a fun time.

One afternoon, I came in from school and the Baldwin was gone, all 800 pounds of her gone! I couldn't believe my eyes. I felt sick to my stomach and ran out into the back yard, sat down under our lilac bush, and sobbed my heart out. I knew, for sure, this had to be one of those heartaches Genie had told me about.

The strange thing, really unbelievable, was the fact no one, meaning our parents of course, said a single word about the piano being gone! Every day we all walked past this great big empty space and no one said a word. Nothing was put in its place like a chair or something: it remained a void. Genie said Daddy must have run out of radios to repair and we needed the money, so the piano had to go. Genie warned me not to ask either parent about it. I was to leave the subject alone. He said asking those kinds of questions would get us into big trouble. Young as he was, Genie fully understood who was in charge of our ambiguous world.

Genie and I missed our Grandma and Grandpa Nelson. One evening at the supper table, Mom told us Grandma and Grandpa had moved to the old homestead 15 miles from Marion in Grant County. They had gone there to care for Grandma's elderly parents, Jenny and Will Thomas. Jenny was crippled and in her late 80s and Will, her husband, was close to 100-years-old. The farm was well past its prime, played-out, shoddy, and downright pitiful. But to a couple of city kids looking for a childhood, it was 40 acres of pure heaven!

This farm was life itself, possessing everything a growing child required for the single pursuit of happiness. The farm was a universe unto itself—open space, green fields of corn, woods to rival an enchanted forest, and a creek brimming with minnows of every description. There were cows and chickens, including a complete lil' family of Bantams consisting of a saucy rooster, a demure lil' hen, and six biddies no bigger than your thumb. There were also ducks, a goat, one horse, several pigs, two dogs, and our Calico cat. The whole scene was one of confusion, hullabaloo, and sheer excitement—a tumble-jumble pandemonium like Johnny Mercer's "Too Marvelous for Words."

In rural Indiana, your barn was as important as your house, and we had a good one. The big red barn was the first thing you saw driving up the old dirt road. Inside the barn were cement floors, a silo, corn crib stalls, an equipment room, and a fabulous big hayloft filled to overflowing with new-mown hay mixed with lovely, fat pink clover, the kind bunnies can't get enough of (Genie and I ate pink clover, too).

Beyond the barn stretched 39 acres of Indiana's finest soil for raising corn. If your corn crop was knee-high by the 4th of July, then you were home free for the growing season. The woods were thick with wildflowers, walnut trees, ash, elm, hickory, and a sycamore. Someone wrote to the *Indianapolis Star* her objection to the phrase in the song "Back Home Again in Indiana" where the moonlight shines through the sycamores, because according to her, there were no sycamore trees in Indiana. But we had one on our farm, and that's the truth. You can tell a sycamore tree because its leaves are divided into five parts, and when the leaves fall, the seeds spin in a slow spiral, like a dancer in a ballet, all the way to the ground.

Wild strawberries lined the creek, and blackberry and raspberry bushes were everywhere. From our point of view, this 40 acres was indeed Heaven . . .after all, what more could Heaven be?

The house, or homestead as some folks called it, was bent and in need of fresh white paint, but the house had somehow managed to hold onto its fading charm, having once, been the fairest of them all. It was two stories, with high ceilings and long, narrow windows. A pump inside the kitchen and another on the back porch kept the family supplied with cold, sweet water from a well that never ran dry.

There was also a good dry root cellar and the wooden floors above were strong and did not creak under heavy footsteps.

Beyond the house were a vegetable garden, chicken coop, pigpens, cherry orchard, and a small stand of apple trees. Towards the back of the fruit trees was a respectable outhouse painted white.

Flowers were everywhere. It was said of our Grandma that she could poke a stick into the ground and vines of honeysuckle would appear shortly thereafter.

Everybody loved the sweet smell of honeysuckle, including yellow jackets, the giants of the bee kingdom. They were good guys who would not bother you if you minded your own business and left them alone to mind theirs, but I guess there truly is an exception to every rule.

One afternoon, Grandpa, Genie and I were driving home from Hanfield in Grandpa's old '37 Plymouth with the front window cranked out. The back windows were down. Genie and I were singing old songs when a large yellow jacket flew in the window, saw my bare feet, lit on the bottom of my left foot, and stung me hard. It hurt like the blazes and felt as if it were on fire. I yelled so loudly Grandpa nearly drove into the ditch. My foot began to swell, immediately swallowing up the long black stinger protruding out from my soft, pink skin. In spite of the pain, I still pleaded for mercy for the yellow jacket. I didn't want Genie to kill it. Genie swatted it to the floor of the car but did not stomp his foot on it. I reached down and retrieved it, wrapping it carefully in my red bandana and tucking it inside my shirt pocket. I could feel its tiny body moving ever so slightly against my chest. Obviously, the poor fellow was merely stunned but without his stinger, he could only last for about a half a mile, then his strength wavered, and he died next to my heart.

We arrived at the farm with our exciting story to tell. Grandma listened as she once again began to save my life with her Epsom Salts and homemade Balm of Gilead. She sat down beside me on the couch, and I opened the red bandana from my shirt pocket and showed her the yellow jacket. We examined him together. He was a fuzzy lil' fellow and quite beautiful. Grandma said folks called yellow jackets "bumble bees" but in fact, they belonged to the family of Vespidae, meaning "paper wasps." He had broad bands of black and brilliant yellow and looked as if he had simply fallen asleep.

Grandma told me these fine, winged creatures did not sleep but rested as needed. She said their lives were short, busy, and very disciplined, with great responsibility. There wasn't any time for fun and games, except maybe when they were very young and learning to fly about. The more Grandma told me about them, the worse I felt. This lovely do-good fellow had died after coming in direct contact with me. I began to cry, knowing he would not fly to his home this night or any other night.

Grandma said, "We can't go about this world and blame God's creatures for being who and what they are."

She was one of those few adults, in my realm of experience, who actually believed animals had feelings much the same as ours. She had an abiding love and respect for all creatures, however many legs they possessed.

I can't explain what the word *home* means to other people, or to other children. But home, to me, meant something I was going to have in the future. I think Genie felt the same, only he had pretty much figured out the details. He wanted a big house with lots of yard and a new car parked in the driveway. He wanted a tall, dark-haired wife with pretty legs who could play tennis and liked to read books. He wanted two children, a boy first and a girl second, about three to four years apart (like us), and he wanted them to love each other (like we did), respect one another, and be life-long friends . . .as he told me we would be . . .forever.

Genie's feelings about home and family were definitely loving and hopeful. Home to me was simply wherever Genie was; the rest was a kind of weigh station, a place to be, until home came back . . . .The truth for me was, as it had always been: Genie was my heart and soul. Genie was home.

As we began exploring the farm, we felt there was something special about this rundown, old homestead. It was bent, but not broken, weathered but proud, standing a bit off center, like it wasn't quite sure how it came to be that way. But from the start, the old place loved us, and we loved it back.

Every respectable farmhouse in rural Indiana had a formal parlor and ours was no exception. The parlor was used strictly for visitors. Ours seem to be lying in state, waiting for God, a funeral, or a visit from the local preacher. It was not a comforting room. It smelled of incense, lilies, Old Spice, and lemon wax.

The dining room, on the other hand, was large, friendly, and open to the sunshine. Lively discussions about the war, the price of eggs, barley, and corn, neighbors and strangers, were all given their due when everyone gathered around the great circular, oak table.

At Christmas, Grandma would place candles in the windows. Snow would be falling, and we'd be eating fresh baked cherry cobbler with real cream. I was put in charge of the cherry orchard and picked cherries every spring. I also helped Grandma can them in rows of pale, green Ball jars. Genie was in charge of the apple trees, which he picked in summer and early fall. Grandma called the process of canning "puttin' up stores."

Genie and I traveled zillions of miles seated 'round that table. We journeyed to Oz, Never Never Land, the wide-open prairie, and even to the island of Lilliput, where the inhabitants measured less than six inches in height.

Grandma loved reading, especially Robert Frost. She liked him because she said he stayed at home and wrote about life around him. Her favorite poem was "Birches." After many readings and talks, I loved it, too.

One afternoon, I asked her if she had been a "swinger of birches." Her answer was a gentle and somewhat sad, "No, but I tried." And then her voice trailed off. Times like this, I waited, not knowing what to say and hoping she might say more. On this particular day, she suddenly said, "But I do know about ice storms and what they do to trees and people."

I confess that I did not always understand my Grandmother. At first, I thought she was talking about folks who get lost in storms and freeze to death. But then I realized that she was speaking of the ice that forms within people's hearts.

Grandma made us each promise to always read poetry. She went on to explain most reading was done for a reason. "Poetry," she said with a gentle smile and a hug, "doesn't need a reason, for poetry is the crown of literature where imagination may experience the kind of validation dreamers dream about, searchers search for, and lovers die for." Genie and I kept our promise with enormous pleasure and satisfaction.

As for our great-grandparents, Genie and I referred to Jenny and Will Thomas as the Old Ones. The two of them were the devil incarnate, as far as we were concerned. They tried on a daily basis to spoil anything remotely akin to happiness or fun, and Genie and I were not about to forgive their wicked ways. I will tell you much more about them later, and it will not be kind, but it will be the truth as Genie and I lived it.

Children may not always comprehend what they bear witness to, but this in no way means children do not clearly see what is taking place around them. (Consider yourself warned.)

Now back to the house itself. At the very back of the house was a narrow stairwell, steep and without banisters to hold onto, leading up to the second floor. There were three rooms upstairs, two of which were used for storage; the third room (and the largest) became our barracks, our command post, and our sanctum from the world of grownups. The whole second story belonged to Captain Dewey Eugene Hall and his crack platoon, me. Every kid should be so lucky.

The bedroom walls were papered with woodland scenes depicting fields of blue forget-me-knots, the perfect choice, considering the secret plans and discussions we had regarding the war effort. (Plans heard by flowers that would never tell.) We were two committed hearts devoted to our God, country, Grandma and Grandpa, and saving the farm.

We had a huge, old feather bed to keep us warm and a tall window for stargazing. We read books, recited poetry, made up stories, sang Johnny Mercer songs, and made plans to capture every German who parachuted onto our farm.

The word *big* suited Genie to a "T." He loved big war, big plans, big action, and big dreams. At home and on the farm, the war was the main topic and Genie was ready with his secret volunteer army, so secret the folks involved didn't know they were in it, and the same was true for the ever-expanding animal corps.

Genie drew maps, made endless plans, and generally organized, correlated, and systematized everyone who walked, talked, and breathed. Make no mistake about it, Dewey Eugene Hall was in control, and as far as I was concerned, the right man was doing the right job at the right time.

One afternoon, as we were returning from a raid on what we thought was a German outpost, which turned out to be a mass of tangled barbed wire and fallen tree branches, Genie grabbed me by the shoulder and pointed toward the sky, whispering, "Look up there, Janny."

I looked and saw a pair of bald eagles gliding above our heads like giant feathered ships sailing on a calm blue sea. They were majestic, true Lords of the sky. We were awestruck, reverent, and grateful for the sight of these magnificent creatures. When they disappeared into the clouds, part of us went with them. We were eager to tell everyone about them. And when we did, they didn't believe us, saying bald eagles had not been seen in this part of the country for years. Not being believed made me angry. Genie said, "Grownups simply didn't have the kind of faith kids have naturally. They have to see things with their own eyes to believe it."

"But you can't wait to be one of them," I reminded him.

"That's true Janny, but I'm going to be a different kind of grownup."

"What do you mean 'a different kind'?" I was confused, which was par for the course when it came to my brother. He was a kaleidoscope.

"Well, for starters, I'm keeping all my good stuff. You know, the kid stuff, our stuff. I intend to be young and old at the same time."

Not having a clue as to what Genie had meant, I just nodded my head and smiled my best "I understand" smile. What I really knew and understood about my brother was he was a straight arrow and the one person I could count on day or night, no matter what. Genie never lied to anybody about anything, except on the occasions when he took the blame and the whipping for a deed I had done.

From my earliest memories, he was always making lists of the things he planned to accomplish in his lifetime. He was forever adding to the list. He kept the list pretty much to himself, but every now and then, I got a look at it. He didn't number anything, but meeting the great songwriter Johnny Mercer was right up top. Genie said Johnny

Mercer was an American original. We sang his songs almost everyday and well into the night.

He wanted to see Notre Dame's great quarterback, Johnny Lujack, run for a touchdown. Genie said Lujack could punt, pass, kick, and even play defense if need be. At one time, Johnny Lujack was voted the best quarterback in 100 years of football. Lujack's greatest game was played out against Army. Time was running out and the score was tied when Lujack stepped back and threw a perfect pass for the winning touchdown, beating Army's immortals Doc Blanchard and Glen Davis.

Genie also wanted to be a fighter pilot like The Flying Tigers, who flew secret missions into China to fight the Japanese. These pilots were all volunteers. Genie had P-40s in balsam wood hanging up in his bedroom in town. He had let me paint on the shark teeth.

He wanted to be a G-Man and work for the FBI. He already owned a Dick Tracy secret decoder ring, which he let me wear from time to time.

He wanted to earn lots of money and live "the good life." He often told me, "Janny, some folks can't help being poor, but I don't plan to be one of those folks."

Genie was a born leader, pure and simple. I believed he was the smartest person in Grant County, probably the smartest person in the state of Indiana, and maybe even the world. To say I was loyal would be a colossal understatement. I was ready, willing, and able to follow him to the ends of the earth, if need be.

Genie's master plan was to save the world from harm. Monumental tasks gave him little pause, and by age 12, he had read the heroic campaigns of Julius Caesar, Alexander the Great, Napoleon,

Davy Crockett, and Captain Nemo of the Nautilus. Genie was a five star general waiting in the wings to be called up for duty.

The basic difference between my splendid brother and me was the fact I didn't have any desire to grow up. I wanted to live out my life on the farm. Everything I loved, from crickets to my cow Reddy, was there. I wanted to write stories about life on a farm, planting a field of corn, milking cows, loving and caring for animals, and how it felt to stand in the creek giggling at the tingling feeling minnows create when they nip your toes.

Deep in my heart, I knew the farm was not enough for Genie. Genie's mind was in a state of perpetual motion; he never stopped thinking, planning, juggling, taking mental notes on everyone and everything 24 hours a day.

Genie was my hero. Whatever he said, I believed; whatever he did, I wanted to do. I was prepared to follow him into Hell and as it turned out, I did, atop the broad back of Old Molly.

Old Molly was a horse, a gift from our Grandpa. She was a nobody horse from nowhere, but we loved her. She was a fine soldier, despite being blind in one eye. She did her duty whenever called upon. But things didn't start out so well. Genie was a winner to be sure, but in all honesty, I have to say that Genie met his match in Old Molly. This adventure did not go as planned, but at least I lived to tell about it.

Chapter Four:

Old Molly

From a purely horse-sense point of view, Old Molly was clearly past her prime, but not so to Genie and me. Old Molly was akin to every horse we ever had, read about, and loved. My favorite was Black Beauty. Genie loved Silver because Silver belonged to one of his heroes: the Lone Ranger. We both loved Roy Roger's Trigger, for not only was Trigger a beautiful Palomino, but he could also take a bow. Genie insisted Black Beauty was a storybook horse and couldn't be counted among the great horses which were real, but in my heart, I counted Black Beauty all the same.

According to our Grandpa, there was but one horse that deserved to have the title "the greatest horse who ever lived," and that horse was Man-of-War. Genie and I knew about Man-of-War because

Grandpa had actually seen him in the flesh. It was a great story we never tired of hearing.

During Grandpa's wild, rowdy, and cantankerous years, as he referred to them, he made his mind up to travel to the blue grass country of Kentucky and see this great one-of-a-kind horse for himself. He hitched rides all the way to Kentucky. He loved hitching because he enjoyed meeting and talking with new folks. His last ride was with a repo car man who shared his ham and cheese sandwich and took Grandpa within two miles of Faraway Farms, where the mighty champion lived.

I'm speaking here, of course, of Lexington Kentucky, the capital of the blue grass state. Folks said wherever an east Kentuckian died, he wanted to be laid to rest beneath the "beating heart" of Kentucky—its famed blue grass, which covers roughly about 8,000 square miles and is encircled by the Ohio and Knobs Rivers. When the wind blows across the rolling hills of Kentucky, the long-stemmed grass bends forward, showing its heavenly blue underside.

Blue grass country has a proud heritage of providing the world with the finest horses ever bred for racing and great horse farms like Faraway, Claiborne, and Main Chance (owned by cosmetics heir Elizabeth Arden, whose real name was Elizabeth Graham). Calumet Farms, as in Calumet Baking Powder, was a farm which held a special memory for Genie and for me.

In the 1940's, families like ours (without much money), took Sunday drives for entertainment. From our home in Indiana, Daddy would drive to Cincinnati and cross the river into Kentucky. On this particular day, we got lost in blue grass country. Daddy drove by a red and white sign that read "Calumet Farms" with a big, red arrow pointing the way. Genie and I begged Daddy to drive up the road, hoping we might see racehorses. To our absolute surprise and delight, Daddy drove straight up to the gates of Calumet Farms. Several people came walking towards the gate to greet us. After talking to Daddy for a few minutes, they asked if we would like to come inside and see the horses. Genie and I were speechless, except for a low "Wow" under our breath.

Calumet Farm was beautiful. Everything was pristine and trimmed in white and red, of course. The barns were immaculate, clean and shiny, smelling of fresh hay, saddle soap, warm bodies, and everything wonderful, which went hand-in-hand with these magnificent creatures. The people in charge gave us ice cold Coca-Cola to drink and answered our questions. We were there for about an hour, 60 minutes that Genie and I would remember forever. Once in a while, ordinary folks experienced extraordinary moments, and this was one of those times.

Calumet Farms had produced its share of Triple Crown winners, among them Whirlaway and Citation. Be that as it may, according to Grandpa, no horse had ever matched Man-of-War. Even today, most will say he was the greatest horse of his time, and some would argue of all time.

To the family who owned Man-of-War and to his trainer, he was known as "Big Red," the most beautiful horse God ever sought to grace the world with, a gift from Heaven, to be sure. Big Red stood better than 65" high with a long, elegant neck, intelligent face, and soft, soulful eyes that regularly melted the heart of every prize filly in the blue grass state. Big Red was a polished gem with courtly manners which belied the super raw power and the huge winning heart only great champions possess.

Grandpa told us the folks at Faraway Farms were friendly and nice to the people who came to see the champion. On the morning Grandpa arrived at the farm, a crowd had already gathered outside of Man-of-War's immaculate white barn. When the groom led the illustrious stallion out onto the grass, a hush came over the crowd. People stopped talking and simply stared in awe at this prince of horses, this trailblazing superstar. As for himself, he stood tall and proud, every inch worthy of his accolades and adulation. He was a deep, red-chestnut, almost mahogany, the color of his Arabian ancestors. Anyone who wished to approach him and stroke his neck was allowed to do so. Grandpa said his coat felt like velvet and his manners impeccable, as one would expect from such a noble horse. He held his head high, nose upturned to catch the pure sweet breeze. He was careful not to swish his tail too fast or too hard, so as not to hit anyone across the face that was trying to pet him. Grandpa said he was mindful of the small children who had to settle for touching his leg, unless Mommy or Daddy picked them up and let them see him face-to-face.

Often, he would lift his head and whinny a greeting to the horses in the nearby pasture. Grandpa allowed Big Red had plenty of friends beside his two-legged ones. Summing up his awe-inspiring trip to Faraway Farms to meet the great horse, Grandpa said it was an altogether prodigious, heart-stopping event. Genie and I had never heard such a flowery words coming out of Grandpa's mouth, but we liked it. We dearly loved the Man-of-War story and knew our Grandpa was truly special.

When Man-of-War died, he was buried on an island surrounded by a moat on Faraway Farms, where he had been born. A statue of the great horse stood atop his grave, just as Man-of-War was buried, standing up.

In 1976, the state of Kentucky constructed the Kentucky Horse Park, the only horse park in America. Man-of-War was exhumed and reburied at the Horse Park. His burial site was constructed exactly as it had been at Faraway Farms with his island, his statue, and his moat. Later, two of his sons would be buried alongside him, both were Triple Crown Winners: War Admiral and War Relic. All of his offspring were champions.

No doubt about it, our Grandpa was an outstanding judge of horseflesh. However, there were times, to our never-ending delight, when Grandpa elected to let his heart do the judging. Old Molly was a case in point.

Old Molly had been born in Kentucky but never had the pleasure of romping in the tall blue grass of her state. As soon as Molly was old enough to fit a harness, she was put to work as a factory horse. Factory horses were made to pull heavy loads such as lumber, concrete, coal, and most anything that required great strength. Horses like Molly were ill-treated, often beaten, and used up before they reached the age of six, at which time they were shot or left to starve to death with their bodies hauled off to the local glue factory.

Molly, born of a gentle nature, endured her dreadful lot in life and did the best she knew how. As time went on, the loads got heavier, and Molly faltered and was beaten. The day came when her legs could no longer make the grade: her back permanently swayed, coal dust packed her ears causing deafness, and sores festered on her body, having never been treated. She was put in the pen alongside the other doomed horses to await her fate. Molly was going to die without ever having known a kind hand or caring voice, except her mother's, who had loved her briefly before she, too, was taken away.

Molly awaited her fate with the quiet dignity animals possess. But death would have to wait on this day because Clyde Guy Nelson had arrived on the scene. Our Grandpa Nelson had many faults, and I have been forthright in telling you of them, but being coldhearted was not among them. Grandpa knew it would cost more to feed and care for Molly than what she was worth, meaning about $25, from the glue factory. But he knew his grandchildren and smiled as they loaded Molly onto his old, dilapidated horse trailer. Molly was about to embark upon a life of luxury, love, and a full stomach beyond her wildest dreams.

Genie and I loved her at first sight. Molly was shy and not able to understand what was happening to her. We led her to the barn. She stepped inside, stopped, and was stunned. The smell of fresh hay, rich grain, and cool sweet water engulfed her senses. She whinnied softly as Genie led her into her stall. We stayed with her while she ate and drank her fill. She kept looking around at us as if she feared we might take the food away. After she finished eating, we brushed her gently and applied salve to her many sores. It was a good feeling to help her. I told Genie that Molly reminded me of a foundling.

Outside of Marion where we lived, there was a big, two-story brick house with lots of windows. One day, as we were driving by it, I asked my father who lived there. He replied, "Foundlings." Later on, I asked Genie if he knew what a foundling was.

"Of course," he said. "Foundlings are children nobody wants, so people bring them to the big brick house and leave them there."

"Forever?" I asked.

"No, just until they're eighteen. Then, they have to go out into the world and make a place for themselves."

"Well, I'm glad we gave Molly a home with us."

"Me too," Genie said, smiling. "Now don't you go crying, Janny. Molly will have a home on this farm until she dies and goes to Heaven."

It took several weeks of hard work, and untold jars of Grandpa's special salves and remedies, but in the end, Old Molly was indeed a whole different horse. Instead of the dirty brown we thought she was, Molly emerged a few scant shades off a Palomino with a flowing full mane and long graceful tail. She was beautiful. Of course, she was still a swayback, but she did stand a bit straighter and was beginning to learn to hold her head up high. In spite of the horrible life she had suffered at the hands of men, Molly knew instinctively that not all human beings were the same. She was willing to trust one more time.

When at last she was ready, Genie and I rode Molly bareback up to the house to show her off to Grandma. She didn't seem to mind us riding her because I guess we felt like a light load.

Grandma came out the kitchen door smiling, her apron pockets filled with carrots and sugar cubes. It was love at first sight between Molly and Grandma. Animals responded to Grandma as we did, wanting to be part of her caring spirit. Molly quickly located the carrots and thoroughly enjoyed her first taste of sugar.

Grandma discovered Molly was blind in one eye. Molly could no longer plough a field, but she could easily plough Grandma's garden, and was proud to do it, lifting her feet smartly, as if on parade.

I felt a deep abiding admiration for my grandmother's way with animals. To her, they were folks, different from us, yet nevertheless, folks. I would watch her talking to her chickens and thinking, sooner or later, the chickens would grow accustomed to their regular routine of corn and talks from Grandma and eventually meet the hatchet with Heaven following soon after, ensuring us a meal. Grandma firmly believed in animals going to their own special Heaven somewhere within the realm of God. She reasoned if the good Lord went to all the trouble to create them and put them on earth, then He would, of course, plan for their demise. Anyway, the chickens never once made the connection and gave up their contented lives whenever called upon to help feed us. Grandpa allowed me to place blue bands on any pet chickens I might have, so they would never become our dinner. Grandma told me animals were here to help us, feed us, and clothe us, but must be respected and cared for with devotion. When they had to be killed for food, she said it should be done quickly, without suffering. I knew she was right, but I also knew everybody did not abide by the rule of humanity by which she was guided. Sometimes, farm life was hard and death seemed everywhere. Hog killing time was especially tough; I was not asked to help and never made to feel I should have, thanks to Grandma.

From time to time, Genie and I thought our Grandparents, Flora Belle and Clyde Guy Nelson, were an unlikely pair to have married. Grandma was soft, educated, and calm of manner, with a heart of gold. Grandpa was rough, cussed like a sailor, behaved like a bull in a china shop, but he, too, had a heart of gold. They were good people to be around, and what went on between them was easy and fun to experience. They worked hard, didn't complain, and laughed a lot.

Grandpa had tried a little bit of everything in his youth, including a job as a roust-about in the Oklahoma oil fields. He had seen his share of monsters to ministers, loose women, and loose hands at the poker table. Genie and I especially loved to hear him tell the story of Kid Sunday. The story was Kid Sunday was the son of a preacher man, so out of respect for his Daddy, he made it a point never to shoot anyone on a Sunday; he did his killing first thing Monday morning.

In those days, every gunslinger was called Kid something or other and most didn't live long enough for folks to get to know their real names. In Grandpa's story, one particular evening in the local saloon, the regulars were sitting at their favorite table, enjoying the game of five-card stud. Suddenly, the swinging doors opened wide and in swaggered Kid Sunday. The Kid ambled over to the poker table and asked to sit in on the game. Grandpa was having a beer at the bar. He said the guys at the poker table didn't look too thrilled at the idea, but quickly drew up another chair and motioned the Kid to take a seat. The Kid was dressed completely in black with his holster tied down, and his pistols sported genuine pearl handles. He was pretty darn impressive, Grandpa said, his tone full of admiration, in spite of Grandma's look of disdain.

Things were going along real fine, the piano man was playing, and the gals were sashaying about the room in ruby red dresses, which matched their cheeks and painted smiles.

"God, I love this story," Genie whispered to me. And I said, "Me too."

Well, things were going along fine until the Kid began to lose one hand after another. Finally, he jumped up, kicking his chair over backwards. It landed at Grandpa's feet. Ever the gentleman, Grandpa tipped his hat to the Kid, smiled sweetly (if you can imagine this), and said loudly, "Don't worry none about me, Mr. Kid. Didn't hurt me at all." Grandpa said the Kid gave him a long hard look then turned back to the guys at the poker table, who hadn't moved a muscle. Kid Sunday started screaming, "I'm going to shoot you, you lying, cheatin' sons-of-bitches, every hog-faced one of you!" Before those guys got to their feet, they were shot dead, a perfect round hole in each of their foreheads.

"God, I love this story," Genie said, slapping his knee.

Of course, we had heard this tale hundreds of times, but it didn't matter, not one little bit. Genie and I yelled in unison, "Grandpa, Grandpa, what did you do?"

"Well children, I'll tell you true and not feel the shame for it. This saloon happened to be the best and fanciest saloon in town. Miss Kitty McCall, the owner, had decorated the place with the finest of everything. Behind the bar was real English wallpaper featuring great big pink tea roses the size of dinner plates."

"Well Sir, I simply took a deep breath, closed my eyes tight and kind of dissolved myself into the wall, thereby becoming the prettiest damn English rose anybody would ever want to see. By the time the sheriff arrived, I was completely gone. The next morning I was on my way back to Indiana."

That was Grandpa, a story for every occasion. Genie and I knew every one by heart. Dad was a great storyteller, too. Folks came to visit on Sunday afternoons and the men would tell stories. Genie and I never tired of listening. As for Grandpa's Man-of-War story, Genie and I never knew if Grandpa really did hitch-hike to Kentucky to see the grand champion, but we were pretty darn sure he did, because Genie said, "While it is okay to fib a little about some things while you were telling a tale, it wouldn't be right to fib about a great champion race horse: it wouldn't be fittin'. Your heart would know and most likely never forgive you." Genie was a straight shooter, and I believed him; besides, it was a wonderful story, even better than Kid Sunday's shoot out in Miss Kitty McCall's Saloon.

Sometimes Grandma would get onto Grandpa for telling us his wild tales. But he would smile and say, "Ah, now, Florrie, let the children walk on the moon awhile. They've got their whole life for travelin' on the ground."

Grandma would shake her head and go on about her chores, but you'd have to be blind not to see the twinkle in her eye.

As for Old Molly, she was destined to become a legend in her own time and in our own mind. To us, Molly was a great horse and "After all," Genie said, quoting from himself, of course, "if you don't know how to pretend, you got no business being a kid."

It's true Genie loved the Lone Ranger and his horse, Silver, but it was Comanche that Genie admired most. Comanche was a cavalry horse, the only horse to survive Custer's Last Stand of 1876. Vic was Colonel Custer's horse that died in battle. Comanche was a soldier's horse doing a soldier's duty.

Genie and Comanche (i.e. Old Molly) had made countless secret raids into enemy territory. Comanche always brought Genie back safe, sound, unscathed, and undaunted in their never-ending quest for total victory over the depraved Nazis. During these special night assaults, I was ordered to stay in my quarters. A good soldier never questions his orders because, for once, the orders were in my favor. Genie said some operations were too dangerous even for his crack platoon.

The fact is Old Molly, or Comanche if you like, was a stalwart steed and in all the years she was pressed into active duty, we only had one major mishap, but it was a doozy!

Late one Sunday in October, during a holiday from school, Genie and I had been on a perilous reconnaissance mission and were hiding out in the hayloft of the barn. We were trapped! Directly below us were two mean-looking, heavily armed soldiers who had taken refuge in our barn. Actually, these Germans were two large bales of hay with milk bucket helmets, holding wooden rifles with kitchen-knife bayonets.

We were caught, no two ways about it. We desperately needed to get back to headquarters. It was suppertime and Grandma's chicken and dumplings were on the menu. Our escape route was blocked by those two nasty Germans sitting with bayonets fixed, ready to slice us stem to stern. Meanwhile, Genie paced the hayloft like Knute Rockne on game day. Suddenly, he rushed over to me and spoke the words which never failed to strike the fear of God in me, "Janny, I've got a plan!"

My Captain carefully explained to me our hiding place happened to be located directly over Old Molly's stall. Genie loosened a few boards, exposing a neat square of Molly's soft, broad back. At that moment, Molly was sound asleep. We knew this because one hind leg was crooked up, always a sure sign of slumber. A good soldier had to know an awful lot of things, and believe me, my head was chockfull of stuff.

Genie was extremely excited; his piercing black eyes were dancing like the sparks off a rocket on the Fourth of July in a kind of hurly-burly hubbub I was well acquainted with, which meant disaster! It was at this precise moment when my knees began to knock and my palms got sweaty.

"Listen up, troops. Here's 'Plan A': we are going to drop down one-at-a-time through this escape hatch onto Comanche's back and ride like the wind to headquarters. Got it?"

Forgetting rank, my sibling connection, and myself, I once again uttered the unforgivable words, "Are you nuts?"

"What was that, Corporal Hall?" Genie asked, grinding out the words in his best General Patton's voice. Clearly, I was doomed, the whole platoon, doomed.

"Nothing, Sir. I said nothing."

"Good, Corporal. Now get ready."

"Except, S-Sir," I stammered, trying to sound reasonable. "Sir, I don't think Old Molly, I mean, Comanche, is going to stand still for such a surprise maneuver, Sir. Just how far down do we jump, Sir?"

"Never mind how far down, Corporal, we have the element of surprise. Comanche is a good soldier and will do her duty as we will do ours. Understood?"

"Yes, Sir."

"Good, I will go on the count of three; you follow immediately. Do not hesitate for one second, Corporal Hall. Ready?"

"Ready," I said, my heart in my throat.

Exactly on the count of three, Genie disappeared down the hole. I heard a kind of heavy thud as he hit Molly's back. I'm sure, to her, it must have felt like a bolt of lightning. She was plainly stunned and remained still long enough for me to follow the rabbit down the hole, minus my soldier's courage and dry underpants. I hit pay dirt and wrapped my arms tightly around Genie's waist, as all hell broke loose.

Old Molly no longer resembled a living, breathing horse. She became a product of Jules Verne, a rocket to the moon. She was the nightmare under your bed. She ran around her small stall, crashing Genie and me up against the crude wooden logs, skinning the flesh off our legs and knees, running our faces through spider webs, wasp nests, and other unspeakable horrors. After four torturous runs, she caught a glimpse of light with her one good eye and headed straight for it. Thank God, the gate to her stall had not been securely latched because she hit it like a Sherman tank and barreled over its remains. Genie managed to duck in time to avoid decapitation. I didn't have to worry on that score, as my head was buried in the small of Genie's back, my eyes shut tight.

Old Molly stumbled out the door and broke into a dead run, which would have given Man-of-War pause. Genie was screaming at the top of his lungs. "Whoa, Comanche! Whoa, Molly! It's us, damn it! Whoa!"

I thought I detected a slight bit of fear in Genie's voice but immediately dismissed the idea as impossible. Meanwhile, I was slipping from side to side; as Molly's back was so broad my legs could not possibly reach around her. They stuck straight out and I knew, without a doubt, I was going to end up smashed to smithereens. Molly had become the horse from Hell, and Genie and I were riding into Revelations, chapter and verse!

My tailbone was now worn to a nub, and I felt myself sliding off. I had a death-grip on Genie and refused to let go, even as he screamed for me to do so. "It's your only chance, Corporal, let go! That's an order."

In my throat were the panicked words, "Are you crazy?" but I couldn't make a sound. Suddenly, we were at the creek, I mean the Rhine River, pardon me, when Old Molly made an abrupt left turn, tossing me first and then Genie up and over into the largest patch of Indiana blackberries in Grant County. We landed as a million thorns bore swiftly into our bottoms, like knives through butter. Genie was cussing but it didn't sound like poetry and not one bit as good as Grandpa's. Finally, he managed to ask me if I was hurt. "Are you nuts? Of course I'm hurt, Captain, Sir. Most likely, I'm dying."

"Don't exaggerate the situation, Corporal. We need to keep our wits about us."

"It's not my wits I'm worried about, Sir." I knew I was mighty close to receiving demerits, but at this point in time, I had lost control. As far as I was concerned, Genie could take his Army and shove it!

Genie responded by patting my back and using his best soothing tones, all of which I had heard before, but what was a soldier to do? I began to crawl forward slowly. Every move was pure agony. We were leaving a trail of bloody polka dots on each and every blackberry leaf, but none of this mattered according to my Captain. The object was to get out of the briar patch, a twisted version of our beloved Uncle Remus tales.

After what seemed like an eternity, we emerged from our chamber of horrors, our clothes literally in shreds, and our faces a red, bloody mess. Genie, ever on duty, reported over his homemade radio that we had experienced unexpected, severe mortar fire but were still standing, for the moment, anyway.

We dragged ourselves bruised and still bleeding to checkpoint 8, which was the barn lot gate. Lo and behold, there stood Old Molly, pretty as a picture, patiently waiting for carrots and sugar cubes.

Genie was livid. He could barely contain himself. He shouted, "Corporal Hall, shoot that horse immediately!"

"But, Sir," I reminded him. "This is Comanche. Your Comanche." The name Comanche calmed him down a bit. I watched as he walked up to Molly to stare into her one good eye and say, "Colonel Comanche, I hereby inform you, you are charged with no less than five counts of neglect of duty and thereby endangering the lives of your fellow officers. You are confined, as of this very minute, to your quarters without benefit of carrots and sugar cubes, understood?"

Molly's response was to begin eating the tender grass beneath the barbwire fence. As I led Old Molly towards the barn, I could hear Genie mumbling, "You're no Man-of-War, not by a long shot."

When I returned, Genie gave me an order: "Corporal Hall, send a runner to headquarters immediately and inform them of the two Germans hiding in the barn. On the double, Corporal. Move it." Of course, I am the Army and therefore, I am the runner.

"Sir, may I request permission to stop at sick bay to clean up my puncture wounds, Sir?"

"Permission granted, Corporal, but be quick about it."

"Yes, Sir. Thank you, Sir."

Sickbay was Grandma's kitchen. Grandma was regular Army. Of course, she didn't know it, but she was invaluable to us on many levels. When I came through the kitchen door, blood oozing from every pore, she gasped and said two words: "Blackberry patch." Without speaking another word, she fetched her miracle cures and went to work on me. The cold water stung but I didn't cry. Soldiers don't cry, at least not in Genie's army. She painted me from head to toe with Mercurochrome, a product dear to our heart. "Hold still, child," she said every so often, but something told me this wasn't going to be the end of it, not likely, no Sir.

After I was cleaned, painted, and bandaged to her satisfaction, she comforted me with a bowl of her chicken and dumplings. A person could die happy if Grandma's chicken and dumplings was their last meal.

After I ate and gave her a hug, I headed for headquarters. Headquarters was located at the far corner of the pigpen. Genie chose this location figuring if the Nazis landed on our farm, they wouldn't want to dirty their shiny black boots in a pigpen. Genie was right, as usual, because we never saw a single Nazi in or out of our pigpen.

Genie crept into the house after everyone was asleep and doctored himself. I was almost asleep, smelling to high heaven of cloves, Vicks, and a host of Grandma's secret ingredients.

Genie didn't say goodnight and didn't complain. He merely crawled into the big feather bed beside me, sighing long, deep, mournful wails of lamentation. Listening to him made my heart ache.

To understand my brother, El Capitan extraordinaire, you first have to realize the word *failure* was not in his vocabulary, not any part of who he was, or who he strove to be. We were a couple of beat up commandos on this day, but by heaven, we were still a unit. Hoping to make him feel better, I asked the big question.

"Captain, do you think the war will be over soon?"

His reply was quick and to the point: "Wars are over when somebody gives up, and no one has given up yet, Corporal, but I can tell you this: it won't be us! Understood?"

"Understood, Sir. Thank you, Sir."

Thank God that was settled. I was sleepy, worn out, and my bones hurt every time I had to move. I squeezed Genie's hand once, and he squeezed back twice, as was our custom. I closed my eyes and was turning over when Genie asked, "Corporal Hall, did you make it to headquarters?"

"Yes, Sir. I made my report; everything was quiet," *including the pigs*, I thought to myself.

"Good work, Corporal Hall. I'm recommending you for a medal."

"A medal? For what, Sir?"

"For courage under fire, of course."

"But Sir, what about me pulling you off the horse into the blackberry thicket?"

"Forget the incident, Corporal, I have."

"Yes, Sir. Thank you, Sir." Boy was I glad to hear those words.

"Get some shut-eye, Corporal. Tomorrow is going to be the big push. There's bound to be more of the enemy out there besides those two in the barn."

Thousands, no doubt, I thought, turning off my flashlight and pulling the covers up to my chin.

As far as I could figure out, war was truly Hell and those damned, awful Nazis could be anywhere. I was feeling pretty sad myself, not so much about our wild misadventure on Old Molly because we had survived worse. I was worried because tomorrow we had to leave the farm. Summer vacation was over, and we had to go back to school. Life in town was pretty tough. I never seemed to get the hang of it.

In my dreams, my Captain was shouting, "Forward, you hard-headed, dog-sleddin', red-headed, sons of a Yukon king. March!" Well, Yukon king or no, this was September and it wasn't snowing in Indiana, which made soldiering a whole lot easier, take it from one who knows. The truth is I loved my life on the farm. I loved being a soldier. I didn't even mind the fact that I was the whole dadgum army. Going back to town—back to school—was, for me, a fate worse than Genie's boot camp, demerits, night duty, and being late for supper.

In town, Genie wasn't my Captain; he was Genie, my brother and best friend—a best friend who took a whipping, a painful whipping, which should have been mine.

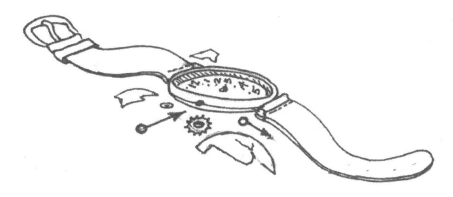

Chapter Five:

The Whipping

There were three things you never did in our house: lie, disobey, or smart-mouth your elders. Daddy's motto was, "Do as I say, not as I do." Genie and I were not allowed to question our father; our job was to do as we were told. Daddy was someone I always yearned to know better. He was the master of his house, make no mistake about it: his word was law.

On this particular day, I was in an absolute panic. My heart was beating so fast I thought it might fly out of my body and crash into a wall. I thought about doing myself in by drinking Clorox, or throwing myself off the front porch; after all, I had sailed off it on my tricycle at age five. One of the handlebars had gone clean through my jaw. I had to be taken to see old Doc Fisher, who stitched me up with catgut. When I heard him say the word catgut, I immediately threw up all over his polished wingtips.

My problem was I had committed the cardinal sin of all sins, broken the number one rule: Never touch anything that doesn't belong to you, especially if it belongs to Daddy. Not only had I touched it, I dropped and broke it! The "it" I'm talking about was my father's watch, his only possession of real value. Our family was dirt poor, as folks were apt to say in Indiana, except for our Mom would never say "dirt poor." Mom would say, "It ain't no sin to be poor, it's just damned inconvenient!" Mom was a blunt, no-nonsense, practical kind of person. Mom's way of talking didn't bother Genie, but it bothered me.

Daddy drove a time-worn, dark green '37 Oldsmobile, which had been refinanced so many times even the bank lost count and had to call Daddy to keep it straight. The Olds was always in Nobe Slovlin's garage, which was connected to his house. Nobe had a sweet wife and a mess of children. I never saw Nobe cleaned up or without a big fat cigar clinched between his teeth. Daddy said Nobe was a Russian but no one knew for sure. Daddy thought the world of Nobe Slovlin, and the feeling was mutual.

Nobe worked from sunup to sundown. The light never went out in Nobe's garage. I loved going to Nobe's place with my Dad. When Nobe would see me come in the door, he would pick me up, swing me around, and deposit me on the hood of any car he wasn't working on. Next, he would get me an ice-cold Coca-Cola from his big, red cooler. Of course, I would say, "Thank you, Mr. Nobe." He'd smile and say to my Dad, "Dewey, you've got the prettiest young'un in Grant County." He might just as well have said, "prettiest in the whole world" because it meant the world to me to hear it said.

Mom said, "Pretty is as pretty does," which for me didn't work out so well. Daddy never said anything about pretty.

Now, I was scared stiff to think what he was going to say about what I had done. Our family, as I have said, was pretty far down on the level of prosperity. We never owned a house or car outright, and we didn't have a lot of things, except for Daddy's beautiful watch.

The watch had a black face and real gold hands and numbers. The strap was genuine leather in a rich, red-brown mahogany. Daddy had been given the watch by the people who worked for him on his assembly line at the factory. About 200 of his people had been working day and night to perfect a way to insert a tiny component Daddy had invented into a radio. It had to do with a new discovery called radar. Radar was not new to the armed services, but was new to Daddy and to the factory. The Air Corps was putting radar in their B-17 bombers and into their other planes as well. The problem was the radios that fed the information were not working as well as they should and sometimes on the way back to base after a bombing run, they didn't work at all. Daddy's tiny invention solved this problem. Farnsworth rewarded him with a $50 check and a Certificate of Appreciation. His assembly line (all three shifts) was given free coffee, Cokes, and doughnuts. Everybody was proud of their part in helping our boys "over there."

Mom later said when Daddy was presented with the watch, he cried. A woman who worked on Daddy's line told Mom about it in the cafeteria. Genie and I could hardly believe it, as we had never seen Daddy shed a single tear. So, this watch was very special. Now it lay in my lap, the perfect golden hands broken, the short hand was nowhere to be found, lost forever in the swirling paisley of the ancient linoleum where it had fallen.

Genie arrived home from basketball practice at 5 p.m. He found me in the corner of our bedroom crying my eyes out. He saw the remains of Daddy's watch in my lap. After handing me his handkerchief he said, "Give me the watch, Janny."

At 6 o'clock sharp, Daddy came through the front door in a big hurry. He ran up the stairs to change his clothes for his Monday night supervisors' meeting at the plant. He was looking for his watch when Genie marched into the bedroom and handed it to him. I heard Genie say, "I'm sorry, Dad. I was trying it on when I dropped it and it broke. I'm awfully sorry." The next sound I heard was the quick snap of Daddy's belt. I hung my head and covered my face with my hands. Genie had been whipped with the belt two times before, and he never made a sound. It was the same this time. As for me, I never forgot the sound of leather as it struck Genie 12 times on his back. I cowered, crying and counting in the corner.

When it was over, Genie walked slowly into our room and lay down across his bed on his stomach. I ran to the bathroom, filled a pan with warm water and Epsom salts. I soaked two towels, wrung them out, and laid them over the angry red welts popping up on Genie's back. Not knowing what else to do, I sat down beside his bed and leaned my head against his mattress. Genie put his hand on my shoulder and stroked my hair with his fingers.

After a while, Genie picked up a book he had been reading about Indians from off the top of a large stack of books he kept next to his bed. He began to read. Neither of us spoke. When it was time for me to climb into my own bed, Genie said softly, "Want to know something, Janny?"

"Sure, you know I do, Genie. Tell me."

Genie put the book down on his pillow and looked over at me. The last rays of the setting sun were sliding through our window. In the midst of the rose-colored light, I could see Genie's face clearly. He possessed the blackest of eyes. Our grandma said Genie had the eyes of a raven.

"Janny, you know the Indians I've been reading about: the Crow, Pawnee, Sioux, Comanche, the Blackfoot, Shoshones, Cree, and Cheyenne? These people were buffalo hunters, hard riders." I nodded my head, waiting. "These people were real, honest-to-goodness, war-bonneted warriors!" I nodded as Genie's voice became a whisper. "None of these Indians believed in whipping, spanking, or hitting their children, not for any reason, not ever! And the white man called them 'savages.' I want you to think about this, Janny."

"I will, Genie. I'll think about it real hard, I promise."

"I'm glad you will think about these things, Janny. Goodnight."

"Goodnight, Genie."

I closed my eyes tight and dreamed about the Shoshones. I loved to say the name Shoshone. I dreamed I was one. I dreamed about tears, too, but they were real. It had been a scary day. In my prayers, I had asked God to watch over Genie and to bless him because he had taken a real hard whipping for something I had done. It wasn't the first time either.

I couldn't imagine life without tears. Tears were always there for you when you couldn't do anything about the problems and fears in your life. I reasoned, feeling helpless was a common condition, as far as kids and animals were concerned, at least baby animals.

There would be more tears to come, of that I was sure, but this time from an unexpected source, my pet duck, Miss Lucy.

Chapter Six:

Baby Ducks and Lilacs

Springtime in Indiana is lovely beyond description. Grandma said it was the generosity of Mother Nature, making everything sweet, green, and clean, filling the days with endless possibilities. Spring was wonderful, but I was more excited about baby ducks being hatched. Most especially, I was concerned about Miss Lucy, my pet duck. I can't remember how long we had been best friends; it seemed forever. When we met, I couldn't wait to get my hands on her, and she took to me like a duck to water! I don't care how silly it sounds because that's how it was. Now Miss Lucy was about to hatch her own wee babes, adding a new line to the duck commonwealth of Grant County, Indiana.

The birds were singing familiar and welcome tunes I knew by heart. Once, Genie told me he had taught a mockingbird to sing Johnny Mercer's "Ac-cent-tu-ate the Positive." This bothered me some because I found this song difficult to learn. Genie told me the mockingbird picked it right up!

Lying on my stomach in front of Miss Lucy's charming abode, I was thinking about how animals get born, when I heard a soft pecking sound coming from inside the egg. Miss Lucy heard it too and began pecking on the same spot. Mama and baby were anxious to see one another.

Waiting is awfully hard; I had overheard ladies discussing this very same thing in regard to their babies being born. Well, from my own hands-on experience, I can tell you it's the same with ducks!

As I stroked Miss Lucy's long, graceful neck, I remembered the day Grandpa brought her home. Miss Lucy had been an afterthought in one of Grandpa's trades. The farmer said, "I'm tired of feeding something I get no return on. This old duck can't hatch healthy babies; they rot in their shells. If you don't take her, she'll be dog meat by tomorrow."

Thank God once again for Grandpa's big heart and his less-than-perfect trades. In the case of Miss Lucy and me, it was love at first sight. Genie liked her, too, and immediately inducted her into his secret Animal Corps with the rank of Second Lieutenant. Miss Lucy was a faithful soldier, and she was a great spy. She could come and go behind enemy lines without suspicion. She carried important messages in tiny capsules attached to her bright orange legs. Of course, my Captain gave her a leave of absence to sit on her eggs.

I sat with Miss Lucy the rest of the day singing or humming Johnny Mercer songs. "And the Angels Sang" was her favorite. I know this because every time she heard it, she nuzzled my hand. At dusk, Genie came to lower the door to her snug little house so no harm could come to her in the night, especially by way of our resident sly red fox that lived in our woods.

Genie, who was dead-set on knowing everything about everything, eased off a bit when it came to Miss Lucy. Genie had decided waiting for babies to be born was pretty much women's work. He had put me in charge but instructed me to keep him informed and up to speed, as he put it, on the situation. After all, Miss Lucy was far beyond being a duck: she was connected, an important link in our Animal Militia. Genie had been trying to secure a part-time replacement for her without much luck. He had tried out a small, pink pig named Ernie, but on his first mission, Ernie had eaten the capsule, message and all. He was, naturally, sentenced to be executed by firing squad for his deceitful deed, but his sentence was lessened to life in prison, which meant back to the pigpen, which Ernie took in stride (and made me happy).

After Ernie, Genie tried out a pair of doves we had pretty much tamed. They lived in the top-most eaves of our barn. They didn't mind the capsule tied to their leg and flew many missions for us. But one day, they flew off into the blue sky and did not return at dusk. We looked for, but never found, their bodies. Genie said he was certain the Germans had shot them down and ate them, which made me cry.

Not yet 13 years of age, Genie not only was conducting his war on Nazis, but he was also the farm's manager. He regularly did the work of a full-grown man and had the calluses to prove it. Genie would plow five acres before Grandpa was up for breakfast.

Grandpa was "salt-of-the-earth," a great horse trader, fantastic storyteller, and simply the most wonderful Grandpa any child could hope to have. He was all these things and more, but what he wasn't was a farmer! Grandpa relied on Genie to the point of taking his advice on the matter of crop rotation. Grandpa planted pink clover for the first time in a field previously planted with rye for God knows how many years. The land came alive again and crop rotation became the standard for our very tuckered out, threadbare 40 acres. Genie had read about crop rotation in Grandpa's own "Country Gentleman's" magazine. Genie was good at anything he set his mind to. He could take apart Grandpa's pride and joy, his cherry red Alis Charlmer's tractor and put it back better than new, all oiled, mended, and ready to roll. Genie loved anything he felt moved him towards his goals and his master plan.

It was hot! The sun was high in the sky, and Miss Lucy and I were still waiting for baby ducks to appear. Grandma brought me out a ploughman's lunch: bread, cheese, and pickles, and if you were lucky, like me, you received Grandma's super glorious butterscotch cookies laced with pecans. She also left me a pitcher of cold lemonade. I shared my cookies with Miss Lucy, who gobbled them up quickly. Waiting for babies to be born was no easy task.

Later in the afternoon, Grandma came outside and sat down on the back porch steps. She sighed deeply, and I noticed it seemed hard for her to ease her body down onto the steps. Grandma never, and I mean never, complained, but Genie and I had heard these long, deep sighs and it worried us. Genie told me Grandma cried without shedding tears. I didn't know exactly what he meant and part of me didn't want to know. Grandma was my Rock of Gibraltar, and everyone else's, for that matter. It was unthinkable anything could happen to her.

Grandma sat on the steps, smiling at me as we listened for the little peck, peck, peck from inside the egg. Although she was smiling, the look in her gray-green eyes seemed to be fixed on something far away, something I couldn't see. Genie and I had seen this "look" before, and it made us sad and a little scared. Finally, in a clumsy effort to bring her back to me, I asked a question: "Grandma, have you waited for baby ducks to be hatched before?"

There was a long pause until she looked directly at me and answered, "No, I haven't waited on baby ducks to hatch. Remember, Janny, I wasn't brought up on a farm. But I do know a great deal about waiting . . ." Grandma's words kind of trailed off. I sat up, waiting to hear more. I watched as she gracefully tucked a stray strand of hair behind her ear. Her movements, like her voice, were always graceful. She spoke gently, quietly, "Yes, child, I know about waiting. I wait every spring for the lilacs to bloom."

Grandma was a teacher, and I was used to hearing her say things to make me think, or ponder, as she was fond of saying. But her remark about the lilacs made me feel uneasy and I didn't know why; it was a simple remark. She looked so pretty sitting in the sunshine wearing a blue flowered dress and one of the aprons Genie and I had bought her for her birthday. It never mattered what the occasion was, if asked what she wanted as a gift, her answer was always, "Well, children, I think a new apron would do nicely."

You never saw Grandma without an apron except when she went to church. Her aprons were smartly starched and smelled of cinnamon, ginger, and pure love. The scent of lilac, sweet peas, and lily of the valley were about her neck and hair. I was waiting anxiously for her to continue, but she didn't. Finally, I said, "Why do you wait for the lilacs to bloom, Grandma?"

"How old are you, child?"

"Almost ten."

"Well, now I believe ten is old enough."

"Old enough for what, Grandma?"

"Old enough for woman talk—talk between you and me and nobody else." I was excited and terribly curious. I felt good knowing my Rock of Gibraltar wanted to talk woman talk to me. I waited. Her eyes seemed to turn a darker shade of gray. She sighed heavily and took a couple of deep breaths. I got up and went over to sit down beside her. She tried to run her fingers through my hair like she did when I was small. But her fingers no longer worked independently but rather in a kind of balled up knot, which caught in my hair and pulled, but I didn't mind, no Sir, not even a little bit.

"I've told you I have never waited for baby ducks to hatch, which is true. I did say, however, I wait each spring for the lilacs to bloom." She was repeating herself, but I didn't want to remind her. Once more, her words faded away . . .soft as a feathered wing. I waited, thinking woman talk was not so easy. After awhile, she leaned forward and looked into my eyes, the look traveled straight to my heart.

"I wait for the lilacs to bloom, Janny, because lilacs are the defense against the tears in my heart. Your Grandpa gave me lilac bushes to plant the day we were married. He knew how much I loved them. You can depend on lilacs to bloom, Janny. They won't fail you unless something or someone destroys them. They're hearty folk and will try their darnedest to grow anywhere you ask them to. Lilacs are a noble species and will grow tall rather than encroach upon a fellow flower. Lilacs don't demand a fancy crystal vase; they are exquisite placed in a jelly jar. If you want to give them to someone, it's best to give them by the armful. Lilacs are tolerant flower folk. Do you know the word tolerant, Janny?"

"Yes, Grandma. Genie told me."

"Your brother is a fine teacher. I'm proud of you both." She seemed to be finished speaking and sat quietly, her hands folded in her lap. She was staring out at her own lilacs in white, lavender, and her favorite and mine, the resplendent rich, deep purple. I was still feeling confused but eager for her to say more, especially the part about lilacs being her defense against her tears. What tears? I didn't want her to have any tears—the thought troubled me.

"Grandma," I spoke softly. "What tears are you talking about?"

"I'm talking about tears in our hearts."

"Do you have tears in your heart, Grandma?"

"Of course I do, child; all living things have tears in their hearts, but it is especially true of us women folk. You'll come to understand this better as you grow older."

"When I cry, my tears run down my cheeks and taste salty."

Grandma smiled, "Those tears are outside tears. Their job is to make you feel better. You do feel better after a good cry, don't you?" I nodded my head, for it was true. "Those tears are good, natural to the body, as the black, wavy hair on your pretty head. But they are not the tears I'm talking about. I'm talking about the tears that live deep inside your heart, so deep, in fact, you may not know they are there, at least, not for a long time. These tears stay inside your heart forever and become part of you, part of your life."

Grandma's word about tears living inside you forever was scary, and I wasn't at all sure I liked the idea. As I was about to ask her another question, she stood up and announced, "I think you and I have had enough woman talk for one day. Come inside and peel the potatoes for supper. I think Miss Lucy is going to wait until morning to present the world with brand new members of duck society."

After supper came blackberry cobbler with fresh cream and reading stories out loud, then it was time for bed. Snuggled down into the big feather bed, I told Genie everything Grandma had said and asked him if he knew about woman talk and tears that live in your heart forever. I should have known what his answer would be.

"Of course I know about woman talk."

"But how do you know?"

"The whole thing is elementary, my dear Watson, elementary. I'm a man, a Captain. I talk to other men. We talk men talk; it's only natural woman folk do the same, though I dare say, on a bit lower level, if you know what I mean."

"No, I don't know what you mean, but I don't think I like it much." Genie laughed his most un-endearing laugh. He had a laugh for every occasion. It was the same with his words; he simply opened his mouth and the perfect words or laugh came tumbling forth. It was amazing to witness this "Genie Phenomenon." I never got used to it.

"Oh, come on, Janny, don't be angry. What I meant is men and women talk about different things. Today, for instance, I'm sure you and Grandma were talking about ducks and life while I was trying to figure out how much money Grandpa would clear on this year's soy bean crop."

There I was again in awe of my brother, who clearly knew everything about everything. I could say it was downright depressing, but I was not allowed to use such a word. Genie had made a list of words I was never to use under any circumstance. The word *depressed* was on it; others included *can't*, *give up*, *surrender*, and *cheat*. Finally, in a last ditch effort to save face and claim some little bit of status, I asked, "Genie, do you by any chance have tears in your heart?"

Genie was silent but only for a moment. I could feel the bed begin to shake and I knew Mount Vesuvius was about to erupt. Suddenly, Genie leapt from the bed, grabbing a blanket and tossing it about his thin frame like a toga. He planted his feet firmly on the bare floor, no more than six inches apart, and I knew what was coming, as I had been in this audience many times before.

Standing before me, regal and commanding, was Mark Antony from Act III of *Julius Caesar*. "Romans, country, and lovers, hear me for my cause and be silent, that you may hear. Believe me for mine honor, and have respect to mine honor, the subject is Tears in the Heart."

Now, you see what I have told you from the beginning: Genie knew everything about everything.

"Tears in my heart?" Genie's voice boomed out into the room, causing the overhead light bulb to sway slowly back and forth. "Tears in my heart, my very own heart? I certainly do not have tears in my heart, nary a one! And I do not foresee having any in the future. Men have strong hearts, brave hearts; men are ready to do battle anytime, anyplace. Men cannot be walking about with tears in their hearts. I've tried to tell you, Corporal Hall, the world is a hard place with lots of sharp edges. A man's job is to carry on at all cost. He has no time for tears in or out of his heart. Women, on the other hand, are softer. They do have tears in their hearts. It is, I believe, quite a natural thing for them. But men, real men, we have 'guts' in our hearts, understand? Men and women are totally different, always have been, always will be. Now then, have I answered your question?"

"Oh yes, Sir, Mark Antony, Sir, and I'm most grateful."

"You're welcome, Corporal Hall. Have you anything to report on Miss Lucy?"

"Nothing to report at this time, Sir."

"Well, not to worry, Corporal. Mother Nature enjoys taking her time."

"Yes, Sir." Like I said, Genie knew everything about everything.

The next morning, Grandma fed us fresh blueberry pancakes, thick sliced bacon and our own special coffee: hot milk with a dash of Maxwell House. Genie left for the barn, and I gobbled down my last bite of pancake, grabbed a piece of bacon for Miss Lucy, and started for the back door. As I pushed open the screen door, I felt a hand on my arm. It was Grandma's.

"Come with me, Janny," was all she said. I followed her back into the dining room. Without saying a word, she walked over behind the pot-bellied stove, picked up a small cardboard box, and handed it to me. I could feel my heart pounding as I looked inside the box. In the box were three large, cracked eggs, each with a tiny duckling inside. All were dead. Their little bodies were stuck to the side of the egg as if they had been glued there. Dried blood and yellow goo covered their small, bug eyes, which had never opened. I sank to the floor and cried my heart out. After a few minutes, I heard Grandma tell Genie to bury them beneath the purple lilacs. Then, she touched my head and said, "Janny, you need to go to Miss Lucy and comfort her."

I got up and walked slowly outside, down the steps, and over to Miss Lucy's house. She was still sitting on her nest; broken bits of eggshell were all around her. She was pecking at the shells. I offered her the bacon, but she refused. She also ignored me. I didn't know how to comfort her, and wished with all my heart I could speak duck.

Sometimes, life was too darned hard for people and for ducks, too. I stroked her neck and silently said a prayer for her babies, then went back into the house. Grandma and I were going to clean out dresser drawers.

The next morning, I ran downstairs and out the back door to check on Miss Lucy. I opened the door. She was resting on her nest, but something was wrong. Her lovely head lay bent forward on top of the broken shells. Miss Lucy was dead. I screamed and began to sob. Suddenly, Genie was kneeling beside me, handkerchief under my nose, saying, "Blow."

I watched in a blur of tears as Genie lifted Miss Lucy off her nest. He was gentle and careful with her head. "I'll bury her with her babies under the lilac bush, okay, Janny?"

"Okay, Genie."

Maybe Genie did have one of those strong man-hearts he told me about, but be that as it may, he had a soft one, too. I believed Genie possessed two hearts, one tough one for the world to see and one soft one for me to see. I helped with the digging of the grave, covering it over with lilacs in all three colors. As the scent of the lilacs consumed us, I realized God loved lilacs and ducks, too.

Later in the afternoon, after Grandma and I had cleaned every dresser drawer in the house, we went walking. Grandma wanted to see Miss Lucy's grave. We lingered there, hand in hand.

"Grandma?"

"Yes, Janny."

"Did Miss Lucy have tears in her heart, the deep ones, I mean?"

"Yes, dear, I'm sure she did. I'm going to tell you something, Janny, and I don't want you to ever forget it. Promise?"

"I promise, Grandma."

"Good girl. You know, Janny, there are people in the world who will tell you Miss Lucy was just a duck, something of little or no consequence. Useless because she was old and could no longer hatch healthy ducklings. When you meet such people, and you will, avoid them at all costs. Have nothing to do with them, do you understand?"

"Yes, Grandma, I understand."

"Remember, child," her voice was trembling. "Nothing is useless in this world. Creatures are of God, same as you and me."

"Grandma, did Miss Lucy die of a broken heart?"

"Yes, she was old, but I think you are right. She had lost so many babies her heart just gave out."

"Grandma?"

"Yes, Janny?"

"I think I have some of those deep tears that live inside you. I loved Miss Lucy and she loved me."

"I know you did, Janny. Miss Lucy's death was the part of life we find the hardest to accept. But accept it we must, just like you must accept those tears living deep inside you. Life has both tears and joy, and sometimes it's hard to keep our balance. But we have to try."

I loved my Grandma dearly, and I loved Genie, but at that moment, I didn't want to try and accept anything. I wanted to cry. Cry for tiny babies who never got to open their eyes and see their mother. My heart was sad, and my head was sad. Grandma put her arms around me and whispered, "Remember the lilacs, Janny."

Later the same evening, we had chocolate cake and milk. I was beginning to feel better. "Grandma, Genie says he doesn't have any tears in his heart and don't aim to have any."

"Oh, he does, does he?"

"Yes, and he means it, too."

"And what do you think about what Genie said?"

"I think Genie's got two hearts, one for strong and one for soft."

Grandma started to laugh, her eyes twinkling. "I know all about Genie's hearts and he's got a bucket full. These men folk are always trying to hide their hearts, it's the way they are and most likely don't plan to change."

Once again, Grandma sounded like Genie, and yesterday, Genie sounded like Grandma: it was confusing. I was worn out down to the nub, or as farmers liked to say, plum tuckered out. I was ready for bed. Genie was out in the barn, helping Grandpa fix the tractor. I climbed the stairs and went out into our room, pausing by the window to gaze into the night sky. The stars were scattered about in a fantastic array of what appeared to be a billion sparkling diamonds. I thought about Miss Lucy up there with her precious babies tucked under her wing. I felt better knowing that they could now see their mama's face.

I crawled into bed, pulling up the blue star quilt I had helped to make. It was to be mine one day for my babies and me. Beneath the quilt, I felt warm, safe, and where I wanted to be, for always.

After I said my prayers, I lay there thinking of the last few days' events. Grandma's "woman talk," Miss Lucy's babies dying before they ever lived, then Miss Lucy dying, too, Grandma's lilacs, and tears that stayed inside you forever. I had cried so many tears on this day, I couldn't tell if they were inside or outside tears, or both. If both were possible . . .it wasn't easy to sort out. If what Grandma told me was true about the tears living inside a person forever, then I reckon mine had just begun their life. I couldn't go to sleep.

When Genie came to bed, he saw I couldn't sleep. He got down one of our favorite books, *Treasure Island*, and began reading. Poor old Ben Gun. He surely must have had tears in his heart.

No doubt about it, the tears which stay in your heart forever are truly a worrisome condition. I was glad Grandma had lilacs for her defense because they never failed her; I had my own defenses.

I had Grandma, and I had Genie. I knew the two of them would never allow any more tears into my heart than what it could hold. I decided I would accept my share but not one tear more. This seemed fair to me in a world where children were constantly trying to keep their balance.

Life was one big circus. I fell asleep and dreamed I was riding on a huge elephant from India. I was wearing a silver dress covered in pink sparkly sequins and ballet slippers to match. My hair was piled on top of my head, and deep purple lilacs were tucked above my ears and in the back of my hair.

In my dreams, Genie was the Ring Master, but he didn't recognize me because I wasn't wearing my army suit. But it was okay because I'd tell him all about it in the morning, and I did, in the car, on our way back to town. School had started up again and our adventures on the farm would have to wait until spring. However, adventure sometimes simply can't wait, which was exactly the case in the story of our famous calico cat.

Chapter Seven:

Sergeant Major Calico

From the beginning, it was "Sergeant Major;" there was to be no coming up through the ranks for this fastidious, fleet-of-foot, fourteen-pound feline, the calico monarch of cat-dom, from the banks of the Wabash River to the shores of Tripoli.

Calico's personality was superior, dominant, wicked, uncanny, deliberate, self-possessed, and unflinching in the face of danger, and she was mean! In short, Calico made a perfect sergeant in Genie's Indiana Animal Farm Corps. Her main duty, handled single-handedly, was to rid the farm of the vicious, bloodthirsty, "blue-eyed," venomous Nazi rats. According to my Captain, these rats had been parachuted to earth onto every farm in Indiana, their objective being to destroy our country's corn supply.

It was, indeed, a giant task for Calico but one she was born to complete. One would never guess this merciless soldier of fish and fortune had been born to a gentle mother in a window box of pink petunias belonging to our neighbor, Mable Tibbits. Mable gave me the kitten when she was 6-weeks old. Mom was against me having her and complained about another mouth to feed. So, when Daddy came home, hoping to get him on my side, I had laid the tiny kitten in the palm of his hand. This little bit of fur, eyes barely opened, trembling from whisker to tail, looked up at Daddy and hissed for all she was worth. When he put his finger on her tummy, she bit him, drawing blood. Watching, my heart sank, until I heard Daddy proclaim, "I like this little beggar; she's got grit!" Daddy was big on grit.

Calico was in, no doubt about it, and I couldn't have been happier. However, as time went on, Genie and I began to notice Calico was not your average, sweet, fun-loving companion. She hated to chase balls, play with string, chase her tail, or play hide-and-seek. She wouldn't touch a catnip mouse with a ten-foot pole, and she never, not for any reason or reward, answered to the call of "kitty, kitty."

Calico preferred her own sinister repertoire of scintillating scenarios, case in point: she would sit atop our old upright Baldwin piano waiting for Spot to come through the front door. When she saw him enter, she would leap off the piano, hit the key of C, and land on Spot's back with a thud.

Dear Spot was part Spitz, his white fur tail curved up and over his back, exposing his immaculate pink bottom. Spot was a fine, regular fellow, smart without being conceited. He was gentle with children and baby birds. It was not unusual to find him standing guard over a fallen baby sparrow or robin until the parents arrived to take over. Spot believed in "live and let live," except, that is, for rabbits. Spot was the best rabbit dog in Grant County. During hunting season, no rabbit was safe, not even in its hole.

Spot also loathed cars. He tried to kill everyone he saw, and as a result, he had been run over, bloodied, and broken nearly every bone in his body at least once.

As for cats, he was respectable, and to one or two, downright friendly. So, it came as an enormous shock the first time he suffered the pain and indignity of Calico's attacks on his person, mainly his bare behind. She would land, dig in, and ride him around and around the coffee table, as I would a horse on a merry-go-round.

Ever the gentleman, Spot let the first couple of times pass without protest, but when the attacks continued, Spot began to take on a pitiful, even mournful, demeanor, as if he could neither believe nor understand what was happening to him. He tried bolting through the front door then breaking into a dead run, but Calico nailed him every time.

Next, he tried sneaking in the back door of the kitchen, but this proved to be a disaster. Calico would leap on top of him from the refrigerator, which was a good twelve inches higher than the old Baldwin. The impact of cat to dog from such a height was so great as to cause Spot's legs to buckle. He'd fall to his knees with a look in his eyes that would cause the devil himself to weep! Genie and I tried everything to save Spot from Calico's constant abuse, but nothing worked. We feared Spot was going to have a total breakdown.

Finally, about a week before rabbit season was to begin, Daddy announced, "I'm taking Spot to the farm. I'm not going to let a cat ruin the best rabbit dog I ever owned." So, Spot went to the farm. The next time we saw him, he was back to being his old self, snappy and in charge. The farm animals loved Spot, especially Bruno, our aged, toothless hound who became Spot's faithful companion. Genie and I were happy and greatly relieved. Spot deserved a good life; after all, he was a decent God-fearing dog.

Meanwhile, at home, Calico had taken a real shine to Daddy, and he openly admired her spunk. Calico would stand her ground with any dog, regardless of size. If any four-legged intruder put one paw on our property, then Calico would send them howling with a bloody nose. Calico was a street fighter, and not to be messed with, period. She was master of 10th Street and self-proclaimed guardian of the finest Victory Garden in North Marion.

Across the street, stood a large, red brick building. It was the home of the Holy Rollers Church, and on Sunday mornings, those folks were screamin', hollerin', cryin', and stompin' like nothing we had ever heard before. Genie was making a plan whereby we could sneak over there and look inside to find out what all the hullabaloo was about once and for all. But before Genie could put his plan into action, the preacher paid us a call.

The preacher wanted Daddy to send us kids over to their Sunday school classes. Daddy made it plain real quick-like that he didn't hold with all that hollerin' and carrying-on, and Genie and I were not going, period.

The preacher tried to explain to Daddy all the hollerin' and carrying-on had a genuine purpose, which was, in the preacher's words, "to rid the church of evil spirits, demons and such, so the Holy Spirit could come in and join the people in worship."

Daddy told the preacher if his church was so full of evil spirits, then perhaps the Holy Spirit would be better off (and get more done) in some other church.

The preacher lost his temper and told Daddy he was worse than a sinner: he was a heathen. Daddy was mad as ever we'd seen him and screamed, "I ain't no heathen; I'm a Georgia cracker, and I'll thank you to get the hell out of my house, and don't come back!" At that movement, Calico leaped on to the preacher's shoulders, knocking his hat off. The preacher yelled, "I'm going to pray for you, Mr. Hall."

Daddy was livid and shouted at Genie, "Get my shotgun, now!" Thank the good Lord, Genie pretended he couldn't find it until the preacher was safely back across the street.

Every Sunday morning, as far back as I can remember, Mom fixed fried chicken, mashed potatoes with white gravy, fresh green beans, sliced ripe tomatoes from our garden, and scallions sweet and reed thin, placed on the table in a jelly glass. We had buttermilk biscuits, sweet iced tea, coffee, and cherry cobbler. This was the Halls' traditional Sunday dinner from day one and of course, if something were to happen to Mom or Grandma, then I was expected to carry on the family tradition.

I have to say, our mother was the best chicken fryer in the world. No one had ever turned down a piece of this heavenly feast, and everyone always asked for seconds. Mom was also a master at killing a chicken. Her method was swift, accurate, and just plain grizzly. Grandma's chickens loved her and followed her willingly, right to the chopping block. Mom's chickens were wary of her, but couldn't resist the corn she sprinkled at their feet. As soon as a head went down for a kernel of corn, Wham! the bird was snatched up and slammed down hard beneath Mom's broom handle. She placed her feet on either side of the head, but not too firmly, just enough to keep the head still, then she'd reach down and grab the ends of the broom handle and give a mighty yank, literally pulling the head from the body. It never failed. After the first time, I couldn't watch, but I waited at my post in the kitchen to pluck, clean, and cut-up our Sunday dinner.

On his second and last visit to our house, the Holy Roller preacher paid us a call flanked by two Deacons and two very large ladies wearing purple hats with shoes to match. Mom was quite taken with their shoes. Daddy wasn't home. He was in Ft. Wayne doing his "secret work" for Uncle Sam. Genie and I watched from the stairway as Mom led the "mission group" into the living room, even offering them a glass of her sweet tea.

The preacher did not mince words. He said Mom was committing a sin by killing chickens on the Sabbath, especially since it was in full view of his congregation. Mom, much to our surprise, agreed and said that she would kill the chickens before church began, early in the morning, which by no means satisfied the preacher's adamant doctrine of no killing chickens on the Sabbath.

Our mother, not known for her tact, got up out of her chair and went to stand directly in front of the preacher. She began speaking in a low, measured tone Genie and I were extremely familiar with, a tone we knew would soon erupt into a holy terror.

"Now look here, Preacher Birdwell, I know I have as many faults as grains of sand on the ocean floor, and if I live long enough, my husband Dewey Hall will tell me every one of them, but killing a chicken on Sunday to feed my family does not make a fault or a sin, and now I'd like for you and your 'holier-than-thou' group to leave my house and not come back, and if you dare say you'll pray for me, then I'll sick the cat from Hell on you. Goodbye!" Mom sat down and lit up a Lucky Strike, puffing away, accompanied by heavy sighs and mumblings.

As things turned out, Mom started killing the chicken on Saturday night, and we finally got used to the hollerin', screamin', and stompin'. But Preacher Birdwell was not forgiving as Christian folks ought to be. Genie and I had to walk 25 blocks to school. Neither of us had ever owned a pair of boots, a raincoat, or an umbrella. We simply had to slog along as best we could in rain, sleet, or snow. Preacher Birdwell would drive right by us, taking his children to school; however, he never failed to honk and wave.

Life went on as usual in the house on 10th Street. Mom and Calico did not get along. Calico liked to play Tarzan and swing on the curtains. Mom would whack her a good one with the dust mop. Calico would not retaliate until days later, long after Mom had forgotten the curtain incident. Calico would wait until Mom was standing at the stove, frying chicken, chops, fish, or beef (at our house, if it wasn't fried, it wasn't fit to eat) and creep up behind her and in one sleek swipe of her paw, rake Mom's leg from behind the knee to the ankle. I can't repeat the words coming from our mother's mouth, but you can rest assured Preacher Birdwell would not have approved.

I was marking the days 'til summer and being on the farm. Genie kept busy with school, chores, and making balsam wood airplanes and hanging them from the ceiling in our room.

One night, an event took place which changed our lives, especially Calico's. Around about midnight on a Saturday night, Daddy woke everyone up, saying he thought he heard something or someone downstairs or maybe outside. Mom said she didn't hear a thing and went back to bed. Daddy made Genie and me get up and stand quiet. So there we stood in the dark, not daring to utter a word. Daddy came tiptoeing out of their bedroom in his striped underwear. In his hand was the unmistakable gunmetal blue glint of his snub-nosed 38-revolver. Genie whispered excitedly, "Holy cow, Janny! Dad's loaded for a bear."

I gasped. I knew Daddy kept the gun under his pillow and took it with him whenever the big black car came from Ft. Wayne to pick him up, usually in the middle of the night. Knowing Daddy was involved in some secret effort for the government didn't help much when looking at the deadly gun. It was all so scary, but Genie found it terribly exciting.

Daddy saw us and said, "I think someone is outside messing around my car. I'm going downstairs to have a look." Genie and I followed like the faithful servants we were.

"What will you do, Dad, if you find someone messing around the car?"

"Hell, Genie, I'll shoot the son-of-a-bitch."

I was stunned by Daddy's remark, but Genie wasn't. He knew Daddy never said anything he didn't intend to back up with action. We started down the narrow stairway, and since there were no banisters, we were like elephants in a circus, tail-by-tail. Calico, who generally led the way in all things nocturnal, was nowhere in sight. When we reached the bottom of the stairs, we could see the living room bathed in streams of moonlight. "Get down, kids," Daddy commanded. "Someone might see you." Genie and I got down on our hands and knees and began crawling towards the big front window.

Dad was bent from the knees, his upper body forward and down in a commando-like crouching position. Dead ahead in front of the window stood our father's pride and joy, the biggest radio and phonograph player Capehart made. The 78 changer had a device like an arm that actually picked up the record, turned it over, and replaced it so that one could hear the other side without leaving his chair. It was the only piece of furniture of any value we had ever owned, and Daddy was enormously proud of it. No one else in the family was allowed to touch it, so if Dad wasn't home, this marvel of technology remained silent.

Sometimes, in moments of frustration, Mom would yell out to no one in particular, "It's a damned shame Capehart doesn't make stoves or refrigerators."

Daddy's reply if he were in hearing distance was always the same, "Shut-up, Edith. You don't know anything about this radio."

And she would answer, "I know it takes up a hell-of-a-lot of room." This scenario never changed.

It was, as Genie explained to me, "One of those ingrained, lifetime structures that went along with marriage." I didn't understand Genie's explanation, but I accepted it as gospel.

The next thing I knew, Genie was jabbing me in the ribs, whispering, "Look, Janny! Dad's hanging over the Capehart with his gun pointed. No, it's touching the window!" Genie sounded agitated. We watched Dad lean even further over the rich shiny mahogany. He was now on his tiptoes.

"Quiet, kids. I think I see something." The next few minutes exploded with a POP, POP, POP, then Dad let out a blood-curdling scream, which made the hairs on the backs of our necks stand on end. The sound, which was enough to wake the dead, was now being drowned out by the shattering of glass as Daddy plunged headfirst through the window, landing in a heap on the front porch, his gun firing wildly into the night.

Genie yelled, "Jesus, Janny, come on!" We raced out onto the porch and were amazed to see Calico on Daddy's back. "My God," Genie said. "Where did she come from?"

"I don't know where that damned cat came from, but I can tell you where she's going." Dad grabbed Calico, put the gun to her head, and pulled the trigger. Click, click, click: he was out of bullets. I was screaming and wailing.

"Janny, stop. It's okay. Calico's fine. Dad's out of bullets." I couldn't utter a sound, but my heart was saying, "Thank you, Lord." Genie gave me a hug and whispered, "Remember this night, Janny. It's a story to tell our children."

During the noise and commotion, Mom appeared in her 100-year-old, faded from pink to white, chenille bathrobe. Daddy looked up and muttered, "I hate that damn robe, Edith. I've told you a thousand times to throw it away." This was classic Daddy. Now the focus of the great miserable blunder had suddenly centered on Mom's bathrobe.

But Mom was on to him, and merely shook her head, replying, "Dewey Hall, what in the hell happened here?" Daddy did not answer. Genie put his finger to my lips so I wouldn't say anything. Meanwhile, blood was running down Daddy's legs, staining the gray porch red.

Mom sent me to get the gauze bandages and Mercurochrome as she and Genie cleaned up the broken glass. Mom helped Daddy into the kitchen where the light was good to check out his legs. What we clearly saw was vintage Calico. Calico had started from behind Daddy's knees and raked him wide open with precision claws as good as a surgeon's scalpel. We decided Calico had come upon us while we were creeping towards the window, and thought she'd like to join in the game, and chose to stalk Daddy as her prey. After all, Daddy was a great admirer of Calico's deadly, demolishing skills, but no more! The next day, Calico was taken to the farm to join Spot. Calico, true to her reprobate nature, showed no remorse by purring and grooming herself all the way to the farm.

As they were leaving, Genie said, "Dad, Spot doesn't deserve this! Calico will terrorize him all over again."

"Don't worry about Spot, Genie. I'm bringing him back to town." As it turned out, Dad didn't bring Spot back, because Grandma had taken a real liking to him, and the feeling was mutual.

Spot, of course, had to be re-classified as 4-F in Genie's Animal Corps. Spot deserved his 4-F status due to his unblemished record in service to the Corps and his years of abuse by Calico. Genie and I missed Spot and looked forward to our weekends on the farm.

Meanwhile, back to the gun, window, and car thieves: Daddy had become a kind of neighborhood celebrity. True to his own nature, Daddy did nothing to quell these stories; in fact, he encouraged them wholeheartedly because he believed every word. The word on the street, so to speak, was "Did you hear about Mr. Hall on the corner? He took on a gang of car thieves who were operating a big car-stealing ring and ran them off. Shots were fired but Mr. Hall winged two of them, one in the leg and the other in the shoulder. He got hurt himself, crashing through his front window in hot pursuit. But he sure did save the day, and our cars. Mighty brave man that Mr. Hall. Yes, Sir, a mighty brave man."

One night, about two weeks later, Genie and I were in our beds, reading. Genie put down his book and smiled over at me and said, "Janny, you know how Dad said he didn't get a good look at the car thieves?"

"Yes, I heard him say it several times. So?"

"Well, I did get a good look, Janny. I saw them as plainly as I'm seeing you."

"Holy smokes, Genie! What did they look like? Why didn't you tell Daddy or the police?"

"Well, kid, I'm going to tell you." Genie stretched his lanky frame, causing his feet to hang over the bottom of his bed. His voice took on the tone of a wise old man. "Sis, to begin with, these guys were really tall, and they were most solidly built, and big, big like the old maple tree out front where Daddy parks the car every night." He paused watching my face. "Like I said, they were big; their arms were as big around as a tree branch and they were wearing dark green, as green as the leaves on the maple tree. The wind was blowing, and I could see them move in the shadows of the moonlight."

"Go on, Genie. Tell me more," I urged.

"Well, sis, these guys are dangerous, alright: like John Dillinger, Public Enemy Number One. Only I call them the Maple Leaf Gang, and this entire block is full of them. A kid isn't safe. Why, if one of those big arms fell on your head, then you'd be dead where you stood."

No longer able to keep straight face, Genie burst into laughter. I was puzzled for a minute or two, and then I got it. The Maple Leaf Gang! I began to laugh, thinking of Daddy flying through the front window, gun blazing, in hot pursuit of a maple tree! Genie and I laughed till our sides ached, and then we laughed some more.

"Remember, Janny, you can never tell this to a living soul, promise?"

"Yes, I promise, but—"

"No 'buts' about it. You can't tell, not ever. Never interfere with a grownup in this way, especially one like Dad." Genie sounded harsh, and I knew that he meant what he said. Not understanding, I still had to promise. Genie said it was part of the code he had for getting along with grownups. "Anyway," Genie smiled, "Dad was a kind of G-man that night. What if there really had been car thieves out there? He was pretty damn fearless with the help of a gun and one big calico cat!"

"By gosh, you're right, Genie."

"Exactly," Genie said, his black, shoe-button eyes shining. "Now, finish reading your book. I've already started my third." I opened my book. King Arthur had found the great sword, Excalibur. I read
on . . . .

As for Calico and Spot, to everyone's surprise, Calico did not bother Spot in any way, shape, or form. Spot probably couldn't believe his good fortune, and neither could we.

In truth, Calico had more important things on her mind, like having several litters of kittens and stalking, catching, and killing the famous Nazi rat, Herr Colonel Karl K. Keester, the only Aryan white rat in Nazi Germany, a personal pet of Colonel Himmler's. Karl was scientifically bred, the only blue-eyed rat in the entire world. He had been created in the evil depths of Nazi laboratories, far below Gestapo headquarters in Berlin. Karl and several hundred of his rat-faced friends had been dropped over America's heartland. Their job was to infiltrate, ruin crops, spread disease, and wreak havoc, in short to be good Nazis. They were to establish the first Rat Patrol of the Third Reich. Karl had landed on our farm and immediately set up his command post in the corner of our corncrib. Karl was a killer who enjoyed his job. At the time of his landing, he had no idea he would soon meet his match: the cat from Hell. When this happened, only one would be victorious.

Genie told me all about the blue-eyed Nazi rat, making my skin crawl. Sometimes, I questioned, but never asked, where he got his information. I figured he must have gotten it from Jack Armstrong, the All-American Boy, Dick Tracy, Buzz Sawyer, or the Phantom. Everyone knows these guys are comic book characters, but think about it: what better cover could a G-man have? It made perfect sense to me.

Late one night as Genie and I were returning from a search and destroy mission, we thought we heard Calico's low growl coming from the corncrib. My Captain took out his flashlight, shined it between the slats of the corncrib and peered inside. I could hear him quickly catch his breath. "Look inside, Janny," he said, handing me the light. When I did, my blood ran cold. Karl, the blue-eyed Nazi rat, had Calico backed up into a corner.

The one thing Calico could not abide, forgive, or fathom, was being cornered. But there she was: her back was up, her eyes blazing slits of fire, her whiskers twitching. Karl acted first. He lunged at her teeth and jaw, ready for the kill. Calico took his hit full in the chest, knocking her briefly off her feet. She recovered quickly and drove her big block of a head directly into his mid-section. He fell over backwards, and Calico was on him, biting and tearing at anything she could. They were locked together in one big, furry mess. All we could do was watch and cheer Calico on. It was an awful sight, but we had to watch. Calico's right ear seemed to be hanging by a thread, and her mouth was puffed up and bleeding. Finally, growling loudly, Calico managed to get the rat on his back with the sheer weight of her body holding him down. In one last huge effort, she ripped open his soft, pink belly, pulling apart his intestines and shredding them through with her fangs. Life was pouring out of him onto the floor. He was convulsing. It was neither a pretty sight nor a clean kill, nor was it meant to be. Calico had met the enemy and done her duty making Genie and me proud.

Early the next morning, with a light rain falling, Genie awarded Calico the Purple Heart. All the Animal Corps attended, including Spot. Calico was pretty beat up and a bit shaky, but she stood proud with her tail straight up.

Later on in the evening, Genie told me he saw Calico burying her Purple Heart in the apple orchard. "Why would she do that, Genie?"

Genie looked thoughtful and didn't answer right away. After a few minutes, he said, "I don't think Calico is one for wearing medals, but she's a damned fine soldier, fearless to the core."

After the Purple Heart incident, we never saw another Nazi rat. They, like all cowards, left their leader to die and ran off to save their own rotten souls.

Calico retired from the Animal Corps and raised one last litter of kittens. She kept them hidden under the back porch until they were nearly grown and wild as any African jungle cat. She had five in all, each one different. They were beautiful, but neither Genie nor I could ever catch one to tame it. Calico seemed to enjoy sitting on the porch in the sunshine, washing her face and laughing at our attempts to catch her kittens. After Calico died, I asked Genie if he thought Calico was in cat heaven.

"Only if she wants to be," was his answer. "But Karl, the Nazi rat is in the fires of Hell, and that's how it should be." I agreed: one problem down and a million to go. Serious problems loomed large, like the problem of the "Old Ones." I was much too tired to think about it.

"Goodnight, Genie."

"Goodnight, Janny, and goodnight Calico, wherever you are."

Chapter Eight:
The Old Ones

Perhaps if Genie and I had known the Old Ones when they were younger, then our feelings for them might have been different or at least more normal. The facts were the Old Ones came into our young lives near the end of their own. I am not proud to admit Genie and I loathed the two of them. They were our great-grandparents on our Mother's side, and they were horrible in equal measure. True, it must be noted they were seen through a child's eye, but a truer picture could not be found. You may judge Genie and me as you see fit.

Of course, any adult would know William Thomas was, without a doubt, senile. Genie and I knew nothing of senility; we knew him to be crazy as a loon and hell-bent on killing us whenever he got the chance. His wife, Jenny, however, could make no such claim as being senile. She was 90 pounds of Grade A mean. She was spiteful, demanding, cruel, and delighted mightily in putting the fear of God into anyone who crossed her path. Up until this point in time, to my knowledge, Genie and I never hated anyone or anything except the Nazis. We understood it was wrong to hate, but when it came to the Old Ones, we couldn't help ourselves. We hated the two of them with the same passion that we loved our Grandparents. This unforgivable hate came in direct response to how they treated our Grandparents, especially our beloved Grandma.

Our beloved Grandma Nelson's full name was Flora Belle, but Grandpa called her Florrie. She was tall, beautiful, properly educated, and possessed a good-size helping of old fashion common sense. Grandma didn't have any sharp edges. Grandpa, on the other hand, was a big barrel of a man, boisterous, and benevolent. He loved to talk and to laugh. He could be quick to anger but like a sudden summer's storm, it never lasted long. And as I've said before, his cussing was an art form. His words could not be deciphered: they simply spilled out in a kind of singsong avalanche of vowels, consonants, and made-up hocus-pocus conjurations known only to Grandpa. You couldn't tell if you were being cussed out or complimented in a foreign tongue. Grandpa was a master of superfluous gobbledy-gook. Genie and I loved to hear Grandpa take off, though sometimes when Grandma appeared on the scene, the lion would quickly change to a lamb.

"Now, Clyde," she'd say in her lady-like tone, and Grandpa's voice would drop several octaves to become a rich baritone, his gray eyes would turn to blue, and he'd tip his hat (if he were wearing one) and say, smiling, "Why Florrie, darlin', what brings you down here?" It's an odd thing to think of your Grandparents as being romantic, but these two very different people obviously adored one another. When they thought no one was around, she would take his hand in hers then place her other hand on top of his. He liked to come up behind her and kiss her on the nape of her neck. Genie and I often witnessed these tender moments, and it made us feel good.

Genie and I had begun to realize something was happening to our Grandmother, something scary we couldn't quite figure out. So, we made a solemn pledge to help and protect her in any way we could. When it came to Grandma, Genie—Mr. Tough Guy, Brigadier Extraordinaire—became Mr. Softie. Sometimes in the late summer afternoons, he'd make her raspberry iced tea, serve it to her, and read Longfellow to her until sunset.

Genie and I didn't dare admit to either of them how we felt about the Old Ones; after all, they were Grandma's mother and father, and she would not hear one word against them. There were plenty of times when Genie told me he was sure Grandpa wanted to wring Jenny Thomas's skinny neck for the terrible way she treated his precious Florrie, but Genie said he knew as we did, that Grandma would not have tolerated any hostile feelings towards her parents.

The history of the Old Ones is vague at best. I can only tell you what I know. Anyone I might have asked about them has long since gone to their maker (this plus the fact that I simply didn't care enough to try and find out more information). What I do know I tell in truth and make no apologies.

Our precious paradise, our irreplaceable farm, was actually owned by Will and Jenny Thomas, all 40 acres. Jenny Thomas was confined to a wheelchair and Will was, as folks said, "teched" in the head.

Before coming to the farm, Grandpa worked at Paranight Wire and Cable Company in Marion, Indiana, and Grandma was a schoolteacher. Both had to give up their jobs, home, and friends to move to the farm to care for her aging parents. It was an extremely difficult adjustment on both their parts. Never to anyone's knowledge, including our own, did they ever receive so much as a simple thank you, a kind word, or God forbid a loving touch or gentle hug, for a sacrifice that would affect everyone's life, especially mine and Genie's. Whenever we tried to ask Grandma about why she moved, her answer was always the same: "It has to do with duty and responsibility to one's own." This she said emphatically, which we knew meant period, end of discussion.

However, one day Genie pressed on asking Grandma, "How long does duty last?" "For as long as it takes, young man. For as long as it takes." Genie confided in me later even the best grownups could be tough nuts to crack.

It's true we hated Old Ones, but they hated humanity and us in general. They were devoid of humor and joy. Genie and I came to many sad conclusions as we bore witness, on a day-to-day basis, the constant malicious treatment of our beloved Grandma by her own mother.

Jenny Thomas was twelve years of age when she fell out of a swing and broke her hip. The hip was not set correctly, so it never healed properly, leaving her a cripple for the rest of her life, a bitter pill to swallow, no doubt about it. I know nothing about her parents or how they handled or coped with this tragedy, but obviously, they didn't handle the accident well. Jenny grew to be a venomous woman who married a man who wanted her 40 acres, so the story goes. They had two daughters, Flora Belle and Nellie.

Jenny Thomas's contemptuous mind grew worse with the years. By the time she came into our life, she was a raging monster who never missed an opportunity to berate, belittle, and scorn her daughter. She was demanding and cruel. Everyone could see Grandma was failing; the more she slowed down, the more Jenny barked out her unrelenting demands. If Grandma sat down to rest, then Jenny would scream and holler at her to bring her tea, fix her pillows, read to her, take her to the potty, comb her hair, or fix her something different than what Grandma had prepared for supper. This abuse went on all day and even during the night. She called Grandma stupid, a brainless monkey, and sometimes even a pig. She also enjoyed throwing things at Grandma or ripping up her favorite magazines.

In the face of this never-ending abuse, Grandma uttered not a single word, but Genie and I took note of the tears forming in the corners of her eyes, which she would quickly dab away before they could roll down her cheeks. Genie couldn't stand it, and one day he whispered to me, "I'm going to kill that old witch."

And I whispered back, "I'll help you." Nothing anyone did for her pleased or satisfied her. She called Grandpa a half-wit do-gooder who couldn't write his name or put food on the table. As for us, she delighted in telling anyone who visited the farm that we were the devil's own offspring and should be locked away or buried alive. She announced our father was a foreigner from Georgia and our mother was a loose slut of a woman who smoked cigarettes behind the barn with the hired hand, except we never had a hired hand, unless you counted Genie and me.

Will Thomas stood nearly as tall as a small tree and possessed the cold, dead eyes of a madman. He was never without his double-barreled shotgun. He had shot at us plenty of times and came close to hitting us on several occasions. Once, while running away from him in the cornfield, the stalks of corn were literally being shot in half and falling over the tops of our heads. The old man considered the golden ears of corn to be his treasure, a stockpile of real gold. Each time Genie and I went into the corncrib to get corn for the animals, he thought we were stealing his gold. We didn't dare tell our parents the shotgun worked and fired real bullets. We knew if we told, our days in paradise would be over, a fate worse than death. So, we kept our mouths shut and our heads down. *Hate* was a word I knew little about, as we were not allowed to use it. We could say we disliked something or someone but not "hate" them. Be that as it may, one afternoon the word became real to me in a way I would never forget.

I was on a reconnaissance mission when I saw the old man going into the woods. I followed him, careful to keep out of sight. He was shooting at birds or anything that moved. Suddenly, he stumbled onto a nest of baby rabbits. I watched in horror as he began stomping them to death with his heavy black boots. Blood spewed from out their tiny bodies and onto the chest of their mother, who was running around in circles. He took his gun butt and hacked the mother rabbit to pieces. Most people think rabbits can't make sounds, but at the moment of their death, they cry out. The sound is human, like a baby in pain. This grievous, unforgettable sound goes straight up your spine, stuns your beating heart, and leaves you shaking. After that day, hate became a tangible, living, breathing thing for me.

Genie told me the old man was demented, but the hate was now firmly in place, and I didn't care what the old man's problems were: I hated him! Jenny, however, was not the least bit demented. She knew exactly what she was doing and never forgot or forgave anyone for anything. She took a keen delight in reading the obituary column every Sunday morning at breakfast. She read it out loud. Grandma was showing signs of the destructive inroads her illness was making upon her body. As she weakened, the Old Ones grew stronger. Genie and I worried all the time. We tried to intercept the barbs and tongue lashings Grandma was receiving. We never heard Grandma raise her voice, or in any way put her mother down. Genie said Grandma was a saint, pure and simple. I agreed. Murder was certainly not a word in my vocabulary. However, the phrases "getting rid of," "doing away with," and "making the Old Ones disappear" were definitely a few we began to think about on a daily basis. I remember exactly when the word *murder* formed in my mind.

It happened on a lazy Sunday afternoon. Grandma and I were seated at the big, round oak table in the dining room, looking at the new Sears catalogue. We loved leafing through it page by page. There was never any money to buy anything, but Grandma and I would pretend we had tons of money and could buy anything our hearts' desired. It was a lovely game. Grandma had a red crayon and mine was blue. Armed with these two magic crayons, the world was ours. Our Grandmother was indeed a practical lady but one who fervently believed in hopes and dreams and encouraged Genie and me to do the same. On this particular afternoon, as we poured over our "wish book," it began to rain, one of those soft, steady, soaking rains farmers love. Grandma had taught me to love the rain. She told me all of nature had a voice, if you trained your ear and your heart to hear it, for no sound was sweeter than the resonance of raindrops against a windowpane on a quiet afternoon. Whenever it rained, she made hot chocolate and a big pot of chili. Grandma's hot chocolate was the very best. She started with a heaping spoonful of Hershey's cocoa, added sugar and a dash of salt so the cocoa would not taste bitter. Then she'd pour in just enough milk to cover the cocoa and sugar, stir it into a paste, then add more milk in a steady stream, stirring in slow even circles and heated to hot but never boiling. When she finished, she added a large, fluffy marshmallow. One sip and you fell into Heaven, tummy first!

My Grandma's prize possession, she had but few, was a Royal Doulton china cup and saucer, hand-painted with glorious scarlet roses, with the rim of the cup and the rim of the saucer etched in gold. The roses' delicate leaves were the color of priceless jade. The china was stamped with the trademark of Royal Doulton, for it had been a wedding gift. She told me she had drunk from the cup but once, on her first wedding anniversary. When she prepared my cocoa, I watched as she poured it into the Royal Doulton cup. I felt like a princess. "I believe you are old enough now, Janny, to appreciate fine things." She handed me the cup of cocoa, smiling.

These times alone with her were so special, words cannot begin to properly describe them, but I knew I would never forget, not ever. On this rainy day the men were busy in the fields, the Old One was sleeping in her chair, chores were finished, and succulent chili was slowly cooking on the back of the stove. I was warm and happy with just Grandma and me, armed with our red and blue crayons, mapping out our dreams while the raindrops slipped down the window in silvery patterns. When we were about half way through the Sears catalogue, the Old One woke up and saw me drinking the last of my cocoa from the Royal Doulton china cup. She set up a terrible fuss, demanding Grandma fix her the same and in the Royal Doulton china cup. I couldn't read my Grandma's face, but she motioned me to wash the cup and saucer, which I did while she made the cocoa.

When it was ready, she poured it carefully into the cup. I placed it on a tray with a pink linen napkin and a slice of buttery cinnamon toast. I carried it over to the Old One's chair and placed it before her. She devoured the toast and cocoa as if it were her last meal upon this earth. I did not take my eyes off of her and immediately stood up when I saw she had finished. I moved quickly towards her, when suddenly she picked up the cup and saucer and held it high over her head with both hands. My heart began to pound. I looked at Grandma, who was staring intently at her mother. I moved closer, my mouth trying to form the words, "Please, be careful," but before the words got out the Old One looked at me, smiled, and then looked at Grandma, all the while still smiling. She let go of her daughter's treasure and watched as it smashed to the floor.

Pieces of scarlet and gold surrounded my feet. I dropped to my knees and began picking of the bits and pieces of a shattered dream. Grandma, who was unable to get down on her knees, motioned for me to bring her the pieces. Her eyes glistened. Tears ran down her cheeks as she held out her apron for me to put the pieces into the pockets, three little pockets with playful embroidered kittens. I filled each pocket with the bits of china. Grandma turned away without saying a word. The same could not be said for me. I walked over, stood squarely in front of the Old One, and screamed, "I HATE YOU! I HATE YOU! I wish you were dead!" The Old One merely mumbled something and began whacking me on the knees with her black walnut cane. I hit the back door running to find Genie and Grandpa.

In the years that followed, I would have occasion to recall the day the Old One broke the precious rose china cup and saucer. About a week after our Grandmother's funeral, I accompanied my mother back to the farm. We were there to gather the things Grandma had wanted each of us to have. She had made out the list on her deathbed, a sad act to witness, but nevertheless important to each member of our family. Among the special treasures she wanted me to have was the Royal Doulton china cup and saucer. Also the Blue Star quilt, a doll from China, a necklace of pale blue stones from some far away place, a leather bound book of poems by Keats, a milk glass butter bowl with a kitten on top, a fan from the 1939 World's Fair, and the small Bible she carried in her apron pocket. Feelings of sadness and enormous loss came over me as my mother and I entered the old farmhouse, but the feelings paled in comparison to the horror and disbelief of what we saw upon opening the door. Everything was gone!

The rooms were empty, not a picture on the wall, or a flowerpot on the window ledge. The dining room, where so much spirit and love abided, was bare except for the pot-bellied stove and Grandma's bed, which towards the end, had been brought into the room for warmth and for the view from the window. It had pleased her to be able to see her cherished lilacs, tiger lilies, and peony bushes. She enjoyed watching the kittens at their play and the mother hens shepherding their chicks about the yard. My mother sat down on a little stool she found from behind the stove and lit up a cigarette. I never saw my mother cry and she wasn't crying now. She was simply silent, staring at the floor. Once, long ago, I had asked why she never cried. Her answer had been quick; her eyes flashed with anger: "It's high time you learned, Janny, everyone doesn't shed oceans of tears like you do! Some people, like me, cry on the inside and believe me, those tears are every bit as valid as yours."

Like most kids growing up, I found the adults in my life hard to understand, and particularly complicated was my mother. I relied on Genie. Genie understood the adults, and he tried his best to help me understand them, too. Genie paid attention to my questions and never once failed to answer them. Later in my adult life, I discovered my Mother had known all along who had done this horrific deed and why; however, she never said, taking the knowledge to her grave. When I confronted her with the name Aunt Nellie, Grandma's sister, she couldn't look me in the eyes, and I knew.

In the corner, behind the stove, I found a crystal toothpick holder, which was chipped. I put it in my pocket and went upstairs. There, in the sanctity of childhood memories, those precious irreplaceable years with Genie overwhelmed me. Spent, I lay across the bed and wept. Why was the world such a hard place? Why were people like the Old Ones so inherently mean? Why did grownups decide so quickly what children could or could not be told? I wished Genie were there beside me. He would have the answers, but he was not here. I was alone in the deepest sense, even though I could hear our Mother rambling around downstairs.

All of Genie's treasures were missing, too. I knew he would be angry. This was to be a day of remembrance, a day to receive the precious gifts of love promised to us that we waited for . . .I had come in joyous expectation, while my Mother seemed not to care one way or another but my heart told me she did. I felt sick and couldn't breathe through my nose. I sat up and looked around the room. All those summers of glorious adventures came rushing in on me like a beautiful breeze; Tom and Huck could have had no better. The campfire circle Genie had drawn on the floor was still there. We had cut our wrists and mixed our blood, becoming blood brothers forever. We had been stalwart knights, as brave and true as Lancelot and Sir Ballamore. We were the Three Musketeers (counting Spot): "One for all and all for one." Genie was Geronimo, I was Alice in Wonderland; Genie was Robin Hood, and I was Peter Pan. Genie was Captain Nemo of the Nautilus, and I was Pip from Great Expectations. We were Huey, Dewey, and Louie; we were "All-ee, all-ee home free." We were children.

Gathering the memories around me like a warm cloak, I started for the door when something bright red on a box caught my eye. I ran to the open closet and pulled out a big box marked RAGS. The word rags meant nothing to me but the bright red crayon did: it was Grandma's wish book crayon. She must have done this while she was still able to hold a crayon and Grandpa had carried the box upstairs and put it in the closet, hoping we would find it. I think our Grandmother was concerned about what might happen to her possessions after she was gone. My heart was racing as I opened the box.

Inside, neatly pressed, lay a fine Irish linen tablecloth, one my Mother had long admired. Feeling my way carefully through the folds of material, I found lace hankies, doilies, dresser scarves embroidered with deep pink roses, tulips, and lavender violets. Finally, my fingers touched two small bags. I knew instinctively they were meant for Genie and me.

Lifting up the first bag, I saw it was dark blue leather, soft as a dove's throat, tied with a leather drawstring. The second bag was made of pink flannel. I could hear my Grandma saying "Pink is for girls and blue for boys." My hands were shaking as I emptied the contents of the first bag into my lap.

Out of the bag rolled aggies, cat's eye, steelies, flints, clay, and big cloudies in fantastic swirls and curls of color. It was the collection of marbles Grandpa had given Genie. He prized them above all else. He kept them at the farm to play with every summer. He never took them to town because he didn't want to run the risk of losing a single one. Even though he was a champion at Ringer, no one had ever beaten him. How could they? Genie knew everything about everything, including marbles! My heart quickened as I opened up the pink flannel bag. Inside was a square of black velvet tied with pink satin ribbons. I untied each ribbon carefully, and my eyes filled with tears when I saw what was inside. In the sunshine pouring through the window, gleaming in their shattered glory, lay the pieces of Grandma's Royal Doulton Rose china cup and saucer.

Genie and I still have and will forever cherish these gifts. Neither of us told our parents about our gifts. It was our own special moment in time. Our life of fabulous adventures and trips into fantastic worlds of make-believe belonged only to us, as did our gifts. Our Grandparents, perhaps without knowing it, had provided us with the time, space, and heart to discover life's phenomenal magic on our own. They allowed us to be children and gave us the world in which to play. Such gifts are priceless and last forever. Genie still has his leather bag of marbles. He told me he was saving them for a grandson he hoped to have someday. As for me, tucked away in a secret place, I have the broken porcelain roses of my grandmother's heart.

The question must now be asked: Was the deliberate act of breaking a prized china tea cup and saucer cause enough for Genie and me to make plans to carry out unthinkable, dishonorable deeds? I'm afraid given all we had seen, and bore daily witness to, it was sadly, more than enough. We felt we must put a stop to it before it killed our cherished Grandmother. Following the "tea cup incident," Genie came up with several unique plans to do the Old Ones in. I was to initiate "Plan A" the following morning.

At the front of the property, where our yard met the gravel of the country road, stood an ancient mailbox never used. The mailman carried the mail up to the house where he enjoyed a glass of cold buttermilk, a slice of homemade peach pie, and a chat with Grandpa. For the last several years, the mailbox had been occupied by a series of harmless spiders. However, at the present time, it was occupied by a beautiful but deadly Black Widow who lived in her web-like splendor, feasting on flies and other assorted insects foolish enough to accept her invitation to "come into my parlor." An Albert Schweitzer Grandma was not, but she never killed anything without good reason. She could wring a chicken's neck in 8 seconds flat if it were needed to feed us, but no pets were ever eaten. Genie and I knew about the Black Widow and never ventured near her rusted tin abode until this fateful morning. This was war, and drastic measures had to be taken.

The Black Widow had become another uninformed member of Genie's secret creature regiment, and she was about to be pressed into immediate service. Genie captured her by placing a cone-shaped metal sieve inside her front door. She ran right into it and was deposited neatly and unhurt into the gunnysack I was holding. My assignment was to sneak into the house, wait until the Old One was napping in her chair, and quietly lay the gunny sack at her feet, leaving a corner of the sack open, a crack to entice the Black Widow's exit. Her instructions were to crawl up the Old One's leg and bite her, at which time "Plan A" would be complete. The plan itself was easy, but my stomach was feeling weird, and I was scared but determined.

You must understand, in the heat of battle, reason grabs the nearest train and vanishes into the night. All you can think about is the objective, our objective, which was to spare our beloved Grandma one more day of torture. After breakfast, I went outside to retrieve the gunnysack I had hidden under the porch. I carried it inside where Grandma was clearing away the breakfast dishes and paid me no mind. The Old One, right on cue, was shouting her daily obscenities at Grandma, complaining about her eggs being too hard, her cream of wheat lumpy, and the golden toast, which I could see plainly on her plate, as being burnt to a crisp!

"Florrie, you are a lazy no-count. I may just as well hire a retarded frog to make my breakfast. Bring me some tea you hopeless old crow." Hearing the Old One berating Grandma gave me strength. I sat down by the window and waited for her to nod off. I pretended to be reading my big, red book on the Arabian Nights. After each page, I snuck a glance at her. On page 110, I looked up to see her head laid back, resting against the gold tasseled, red, white, and blue pillow of the United States Air Force. She was sound asleep and snoring. I quickly lifted up one corner of the gunnysack. Out leapt the Black Widow on her eight little hairy legs, propelling herself directly onto the black booted leg of the Old One.

I watched, transfixed, as our secret weapon scurried to reach her objective, the pure white skin of the Old One's neck. I couldn't move until I felt the hand of God tapping me on the shoulder. I heard a voice say, "What do you think you're doing, Missy?" I opened my mouth and screamed to high heaven. Dishes clattered to the floor, the Old One woke up and began whacking me on the head and back with her cane shouting, "What are you doing you devil child? Get that filthy duck out of this house or I'll kill it!"

Duck, what duck? In the wild confusion with God speaking to me and all the rest, I hadn't seen Harvey—Miss Lucy's friend—enter the room. I quickly grabbed him up into my arms, and to my never-ending horror saw two black hairy legs protruding from his bright orange beak. Genie's perfect plan had not taken into account the surprise visit of Harvey, who had missed Miss Lucy and went looking for her. He hadn't found Miss Lucy but he found lunch scampering up the body of the Old One. In one amazingly quick movement, "Plan A" was gone and a valuable secret weapon right along with it. I was in a state of woe-is-me, big time! Like the coward I was, I stumbled out the back door, dropping a satisfied Harvey to the ground. I could hear the Old One yelling at Grandma, who was no doubt trying to sort out what had happened.

The sun felt unusually hot on my face. I could care less. I lay down on the grass thinking *this is hell*; I fully expected the hand of God to reach down from Heaven and strike me dead. Genie came running up from the orchard quite out of breath. "Well, Corporal, how did it go? Did you execute 'Plan A' correctly?"

Slowly, I managed to rise to a sitting position and saluted as best I could. "Well Sir, Captain, Sir . . . ." I was having a terrible time getting my words out.

"What's wrong with you, Corporal? Your cheeks are fire engine red while the rest of you is as pale as a ghost. Speak up, Corporal Hall. Pull yourself together, Marine. SPEAK!"

"Well, Sir, I'm afraid 'Plan A' didn't go exactly as planned, Sir. In fact, it barely went at all." I hung my head, dreading to look my Captain in the eye.

"My God, Janny, I mean, Corporal Hall, are you telling me our secret weapon is running loose in the house?" Genie sounded extremely jittery.

"No, Sir, what I'm saying, is our secret weapon, the Black Widow, is dead, Sir." "Dead, Sir? How, Sir?" We were beginning to sound like Abbott and Costello. "Genie, I mean, Captain Sir, I was taken by surprise."

"Surprise? Explain yourself, Corporal Hall."

"Well, Sir, 'Plan A' was going along fine until Harvey arrived. I didn't see him until it was too late. Harvey saw the Black Widow dashing up the leg of our enemy and ZAP, our secret weapon was gone!"

"Damn that duck!" Genie shouted, then seeing the tears running down my cheeks, he lowered his voice and said, "It's all right, Janny, you did the best you could. I won't punish Harvey for being who he is, regardless of the fact he heads-up the only duck resistance unit in this man's Army. Even the best units have flaws." I sighed a sigh of relief knowing Harvey would not be brought up on charges. Genie sat down on the grass beside me; he was eating an apple. He sliced off a piece with his hunting knife and offered it to me saying, "None of this is your fault, Corporal Hall, and don't worry, we'll take care of the Old One another time. Meanwhile, I've got 'Plan B' nearly ready to go."

I simply couldn't tell Genie I had chickened out at the last minute and screamed to alert the Old One. Why was life so darn complicated, and why was it left up to us to fix it? I knew the answer: we were on a mission to save our Grandmother, which was all that mattered. "Are you listening, Corporal Hall?" Genie's voice snapped me back into the reality of the moment.

"Yes, Sir, all ears, Sir."

"Good, now listen up while I tell you about 'Plan B.' I've been watching the old man for days and I know his routine. You know the hollow tree in the apple orchard, Corporal?"

"Yes, Sir, the tree where Calico hid her kittens."

"The very one, well, Corporal the hollow tree has become the new hiding place for the old man's gold. The tree is nearly filled to the top of the hollow space with corncobs, his precious bars of gold. He shows up three nights a week, just as it's getting dark. The next time he shows, I'll be waiting." Genie was pacing to-and-fro, squinting his eyes, and looking serious.

"And then what?" I asked somewhat timidly.

"I've been busy, Corporal Hall. I've been digging. I've dug a large, deep hole in front of the hollow tree and covered it over with pine branches. When he comes with a fresh load of his corncob gold, I'll leap out from behind the tree and scare the pants off him. When he drops the gold and turns to run, he'll fall right into the hole." Genie hesitated, lowering his voice to a whisper and in a tone of pure glee stated: "And then we will be rid of that giant butcher of baby rabbits."

"But what if the fall doesn't do him in?" I had to ask the question.

"Doesn't kill him, you mean?"

"Yes, that's what I mean, alright."

"Janny, I mean, Corporal Hall, the man is older than God. It will be curtains for him; I guarantee it. Now stop worrying; this is what we'll do. First, we take turns staking out the hollow tree. He's bound to return soon with another armload of gold. He's a greedy old bastard and a miser, too; it's all he thinks about."

"Yeah, and killing us with his shotgun."

"Not this time, Corporal Hall; this time we'll be waiting for him." As it turned out, we kept our vigil for three nights, sleeping on the ground near the hollow tree next to the pigpen. The night air was chilly, and the sweet smell of apples hardly mixed with the unmistakable odor of piggies at rest. Our passionate cause was not to bear fruit because the old man never showed his face. Perhaps he had forgotten his hiding place or worse, found a new one. Genie was fit to be tied, I was just plain worn out, and neither of us smelled like roses. Finally, after much pacing and hand wringing on Genie's part, it was decided we should sleep in our own bed. Boy was I glad. The old feather bed never felt so good. Genie hardly slept, as he was now keeping watch from our window. This seemed silly to me because the window faced the road. If you stood sideways, then you might be able to see a small sliver of the hollow tree area.

Genie was not one to give up or give in; he reminded me of the tenacious Boston Bull Terrier named Blackie, who lived next door to us in town on Adams Street. Blackie would grab hold of tin cans he found in the trash barrel, and you could lift him up into the air and swing him 'round and 'round, but he would not let go of his can.

To continue, on the fourth night we were wakened by the fiendish screams of some monster, beast, or Nazi invading our territory. Right here, I will tell you a simple truth about the difference between my illustrious brother and me. When we heard the heart stopping piercing cry, my blood ran cold while Genie's ran hot. For Genie, once again, the game was afoot, and he was knee deep in his element. "Genie," I cried out, "what's that sound?" Genie didn't answer but flew out of bed like some wild bird released from its cage.

"Janny, come on, grab your shoes! Be quiet; be quick; there's not a moment to lose." We tiptoed down the stairs. The house was silent. The Old Ones slept at the other end of the house, as did our grandparents, so they could be near them in case they needed help during the night. We ran out the back door, leaving it slightly ajar.

Within minutes, we were climbing over the fence into the apple orchard, why I don't know, as there was, of course, a perfectly good gate. But that was my leader, my brother, the consummate commando who was over fences, climbing walls, rain or shine, night or day. You had to admire this fellow; I surely did. As we neared the hole, the sounds were less high-pitched but just as scary.

Suddenly, Genie grabbed both my hands and whispered, "Fee Fie Foe Fum, I smell the blood of a Nazi. Be him alive or be him dead, I'll grind his bones to make my bread."

"Genie, for God's sake, you're scaring me. I'm going back to the house."

"Corporal Hall." Genie commanded.

"Yes, Sir?" I responded; how could I not? I had been so well trained.

"Man your post, Corporal."

"What post, Sir?"

"This post, Corporal Hall," Genie said placing my hand on the wooden post holding up the fence. "Stay put, Corporal, and I'll move forward to see what we have trapped and find out if the shotgun is with the prisoner." I was happy to stay glued to the post. The next thing I heard was a big gasp followed by long, lingering, heartrending moans. My heart was in danger of quitting all together when I heard Genie's voice in a kind of agonizing wail.

"Oh, no! Oh, my God, no! No, no!" Genie seemed to be pleading to God himself.

Not being able to listen one second longer, I ran to his side. He was rolling about on the ground in the moonlight, mumbling words I couldn't understand.

"Genie, what is it? What's wrong? Are you alright?"

"No, I'm not alright, Corporal Hall. Take a look inside the hole." Seeing my General in a state of full-blown heebie-jeebies, I knew that we were dead. Not knowing what else to do, I bent down and peered into the hole. There was just enough moonlight to make out the silhouette of a big, fat body.

"Oh, my stars, Genie! I mean, Captain Sir, it's not the old man: it's Grandpa's brand new Hampshire hog!" It was one of his better trades and now it was in the bottom of a hole meant for the Old One.

"I know, I know," Genie moaned, still rolling about holding his head. He looked like a crazy person I had once seen at the county fair. Grandpa said the man had fallen into a fit, and I was not to look, but I did.

"Genie, have you fallen into a fit?" I was so frightened. Genie didn't answer but continued moaning. I felt desperate and blurted out, "Don't worry, Genie, we'll get him out of there before the sun comes up." This seemed like the right solution to me.

All at once, Genie sat up straight and said, "Brilliant, my dear Watson, but how? Now there's the trick, my old friend."

Being Genie's sister, Marine spy, comrade in arms, and soul mate was never an easy role. It was exciting but never easy. I had no idea how we were going to get a huge pig out of this deep hole.

Genie was one his feet shouting, "Corporal Hall!"

"Yes, Sir?" I replied, wondering what he would say or do next.

"Corporal, do you have any idea what this pig weighs?"

"No, Sir, but I—"

"No 'buts' about it, Corporal. This pig weighs 250 pounds if he weighs an ounce. He may even weigh 350 pounds—who knows? We are in deep water, Corporal, and it's getting deeper all the time. We may be doomed . . . I repeat: doomed."

It was unsettling to hear those words coming from Genie, who knew everything about everything and never gave up. I was scared for Genie, for myself, and hey, I was even scared for the pig! What a mess! Not only had "Plan A" failed, but "Plan B" had run amuck, and we had no plan for this new, tragic development—prize pig in a hole.

There was no joy in Mudville; Genie and I had struck out.

I sat in the grass, watching Genie pace back and forth and listening to the pig put in his two cents worth. I wondered if this night would ever end. After what seemed an eternity, Genie shouted, "I've got a plan!"

I could tell Genie was terribly excited about this plan. "I know it will work, Janny, because it involves Grandpa, and Grandpa is a sport, a good guy. All we have to do is be honest, straightforward, and meet the problem head-on."

Somehow, hearing Genie's plan did not set my mind at ease, especially the word *straightforward*. And bringing in grownups, even a beloved one, had always been strictly taboo. I knew Grandpa was a sport, and I loved him dearly. We also knew he was aware of Genie's farm militia. In fact, he seemed to get a kick out of it. Maybe Genie was onto something; he had to be—he was Genie, El Captain, Sherlock Holmes, and the Green Hornet, all rolled into one.

The plan began with another sleepover by the hole. According to my leader, the prize pig was now our prisoner: overnight he had become a Nazi pig! At daybreak, we ran to the house and up the stairs to put on our makeshift uniforms over our pajamas, for time was of the essence. We grabbed our Army surplus helmets, canteens, and wooden rifles. We were ready to march.

Since we didn't have far to go, we marched double-time straight to the barn where we found Grandpa mixing feed. He broke into a big grin when he saw us coming. Genie, his back stiff as a board, gave Grandpa a snappy salute. "Good morning, Mr. Nelson. I'm Captain Hall."

"Of course you are, son," Grandpa said, playing along. "What can I do for you, Captain?"

"Well, sir, it's what I can do for you: that's the question."

"Sounds a might interesting, Captain. What is it that you can do for me?"

"Sir, my Corporal and I," Genie said, motioning to me. I waved at Grandpa and smiled my sweetest smile, the smile Genie taught me to use on grownups. "We have captured a German officer in your apple orchard."

"In my apple orchard? Now that is news! Who's guarding this dangerous German officer? Is he one of those Nazis?"

"Yes, he is: he's a Nazi pig, sir. As for who's guarding him, I will have to say no one, but you can rest easy because he is trapped and can't escape. No, sir, he can't get free from where he is, sir."

I couldn't help but notice Genie was shifting first to one foot and then to the other, a sure sign he needed my help, so I chimed in,

"The prisoner is in our foxhole, Grandpa, I mean, Mr. Nelson, sir, and we dig our foxholes really deep. There is no way he can get out." I glanced over at Genie, and he winked at me. I knew I had said the right thing.

"Well, troops, it would seem you have the situation well in hand, but perhaps I'd better have a look at this vile fellow myself. Will you lead the way, Captain Hall?"

"Yes, sir, gladly, sir." The three of us fell into step and off we headed to the apple orchard. By now, the sun was high and shining brightly. I didn't allow myself to think about what might happen when Grandpa looked into that hole; I just kept putting one foot in front of the other and crossing all the fingers I could. We reached the hole all too soon for me. I had to use all my military training to keep from running away.

Grandpa had a puzzled look on his face as we walked up to the hole. No doubt, he had heard the plaintive sounds of the prisoner. He walked to the edge, peered over, and in that moment, the world ceased to move. I couldn't bear to look at Genie and kept my eyes on the ground. The silence was simply unbearable until suddenly Grandpa burst into his big, booming, bodacious laughter, which literally shook the ground where we stood. Genie and I, still not breathing properly, embraced the sound of Grandpa's laughter: it was music to our ears!

In the hearty throes of lifesaving laughter, Grandpa said, "Ugly fellow, ain't he? Kind of puts me in the mind of a big, fat Hampshire hog. What do you think, Captain Hall?"

"Oh, yes, sir. He's ugly, alright, and plenty fat, too." Genie was beginning to laugh nervously. I started to laugh, too, a high-pitched totally ridiculous kind of laugh. Meanwhile, Grandpa continued laughing so hard he had to bend over; he finally sat down on the grass and slapped his knees in what seemed to be total glee.

In the end, the three of us went a little crazy. There aren't words funny enough to explain the way laughter can take over your heart and cause it to leap like a lamb in springtime; your mind tosses away its worries; you relax and feel free. Everything is wonderful; hope is restored. Laughter is about the best thing there is, especially to kids.

Grandpa never asked us a single question, instead he showed us how to make something he called a "sluice." It was a series of soft dirt steps smoothed out to make a slide. The slide was spread with lettuce, apples, last night's biscuits, fresh corn, and some pieces of carrots. Well, all I can tell you is when the Nazi pig spied those goodies, he stood up, snorted, and grunted his way up the sluice without so much as a bobble. Genie, of course, was waiting for him and forced him back into the pigpen, which had become our prisoner of war camp. Grandpa, still chuckling, congratulated us on our valor and asked that we keep up the vigil. You can bet we promised (most gratefully) for as long as it took, until the war was won.

During the next two years, the Old Ones died of pure meanness and old age. The old man died in his bed; under his mattress, we found the rest of his precious gold: over 300 ears of dried corn. As was the custom of the day, both their wakes were held at home in the front parlor. On both occasions, Genie and I snuck downstairs to view our enemies. Each time we found copper pennies had been placed on their eyes, and each time, Genie removed the pennies, took them outside, and threw them as far as he could. When I asked him why, he replied,

"Those two old buzzards are on their way to Hell, Janny, and I don't want them to miss a single thing on their way down or have any money when they get there!"

After their death, neither Genie nor I ever spoke about the Old Ones. I don't think either of us felt good about our plans to get rid of them. But having to witness the daily destruction of someone you hold most dear was more than we had been able to bear. We were not the devil's children: we felt we had to do whatever we could to save our Grandmother from an early grave, but in the end, nothing could save her.

Genie told me when God was made aware of all the facts in the case we would be forgiven. Children believe things because their hearts tell them to; I believed it because Genie told me it was true.

Once again, summer had ended, a crushing blow to me. If only I could become invisible or turn into a bird by Merlin's magic and simply fly far, far away . . . .But, of course, nothing was going to save me except Genie, one more time. Although, this time, Genie would enlist the help of an Indian brave called Geronimo.

Chapter Nine:

Geronimo and the Last Snowball

Geronimo was a full-blooded Chiricahua Eastern Apache who fought and led his people during the latter half of the 19th century. The Chiricahua were known to be the most nomadic and aggressive of all the tribes that made up the Eastern and Western Apache. Geronimo was the last great Indian leader to be captured in 1886.

At one time, Apache land stretched from east central and southwestern Arizona, Colorado, New Mexico, and western Texas to Sonora. After Geronimo was captured, he and his people were held as prisoners of war and sent to Florida, Alabama, and Fort Sill, Oklahoma for a total of 27 years. The name "Geronimo" means "The Smart One." Geronimo was one of Genie's heroes. Genie told me the Indians were doomed to defeat from the start by a single word: *progress.*

In my small, insular world, progress didn't mean much. I was on the side of the Indian every time. I, like them, didn't like change; I feared it. I wanted to live on the farm forever, to leave school and live my life amidst the cornfields, pastures, and animals. The farm was home. I loved farm life and dreaded going back to town each September. School terrified me, and on this unforgiving day, the terror was more than I could handle. I needed a miracle, and I got one in the form of Geronimo, a paler version to be sure, but nonetheless true as true can be.

It was a wintry Indiana day, cold to the bone, as farmers would say. I was walking home from school. The snow was coming down hard in great, chunky flakes that stuck to my long, black braids like glue. Kids at school called me "Dirty Indian" or "Pocahontas Puke." I was a skinny, scared rabbit of a kid who couldn't understand or handle teasing, much less fight back. Without Genie, I was afraid of everything and everybody. I was especially frightened of the boy who was following me.

He was a bully, a sixth-grader. I had seen him beating up on smaller kids and taking their lunch money. I remembered his red hair and pointed toe cowboy boots because nobody wore cowboy boots in Indiana.

He had been following me for several days and getting bolder all of the time, calling me names and throwing stingers at me. Stingers were snowballs packed tight with rocks and cinders. Genie and I had never owned a pair of boots of any kind. Our shoes were always wet clean through to our frozen toes by the time we had trudged the twenty-five blocks from school to home.

I wanted to run in the worst way, but I knew he would catch me. I was scared stiff and feared I'd wet my pants. Finally, I couldn't stand it one minute longer, and I took off running. My worst fears were quickly realized. The bully was on me in an instant, leaping onto my back as you would leap onto a horse. I screamed, but the sheer weight of his body knocked the breath out of me, and I crashed to the ground.

I felt a stab of sharp pain as his knee rammed into the small of my back. I felt his hands on the back of my neck, forcing my face down into the freezing snow. The snow stung my cheeks like #7 sandpaper. I began to taste my own blood; it seemed to be pouring out of my nose and mouth. Soon, the snow around my face had turned a deep crimson, and I did wet my pants.

He was laughing at my cries begging him to stop. He was riding me like a horse, screaming, "You dimwitted, bird brained, Indian. I'm going to beat the shit out of you and make you disappear." And I did; I disappeared into the bottom of the snow bank. I could taste gravel, dirt, and frozen leaves mixed up with the bloody snow. I didn't move: I thought I had died! He kicked me in the side, but I didn't make a sound. Playing possum worked because he raised himself up and got off of me; game over; he won. I watched as he slowly swaggered off down the street. I sat up but still couldn't breathe properly. But he was gone; my enemy was gone. I felt my face, and it was a sticky, bloody mess. I was glad my coat was red. I didn't like red, but maybe the bloodstains wouldn't show.

I was hurting all over but kept plodding along until at last, I saw my house. What a crummy old rattrap it was, too—one of the many we had moved in and out of like birds going from nest to nest. These houses were always besides railroad tracks. Our house was so close to the tracks that when the Super Chief roared by at midnight, Genie's bed and mine would slide out from opposites sides of the room and meet in the middle. At this point, Genie would jump up, give a snappy salute, and sing, "Hail to the Chief."

It never seemed to bother Genie what kind of horrible house we lived in; he would somehow make it seem okay. However, he did mind not having proper boots. He'd say, "It's a damn shame we don't have any boots! A Marine has got to have boots."

"That's for damned sure," I'd always chime in at this point. Genie would allow my cussing, and I wouldn't even receive a demerit.

Usually, he'd follow up by saying, "Buck up, kid. The next house can't possibly be any worse; the odds are in our favor."

"How?" Sometime I didn't get the message.

"That's easy: this house is the bottom rung: the next step is up."

Besides our dancing beds, this house had one very strange feature: the kitchen had a door in the floor that took up most of the room. The door had a knob from which a rope was tied, stretched, and then fastened to a large hook in the ceiling. This "floor door" led to the basement. To enter the basement, you first had to move the kitchen table and chairs. Every house we rented had a dark, dank basement with a huge old coal furnace that never seemed to work.

Genie's job was to keep the furnace stoked with coal because there was hell to pay if the fire ever went out. My job, and Genie's, too, was to walk the railroad tracks picking up the pieces of slag coal that fell from B&O's heavily laden freight cars hauling coal. I never went down to the basement without remembering our first Thanksgiving in that house.

A few days prior to my snowball terror, Daddy rushed in from the factory all excited about the great deal he'd gotten on a turkey for our holiday feast. It was to be delivered the day before Thanksgiving. Daddy was very proud of his deal, and Genie and I were happy knowing we wouldn't have to eat stewed rabbit.

As promised, the turkey arrived the day before Thanksgiving. The problem was the turkey arrived alive, big, and brassy—feathers and all! Genie and I laughed so hard we nearly made ourselves sick. We secured Tom Turkey to the porch railing and sat down to wait. We knew feathers were going to fly in more ways than one.

Mom got off work at four in the afternoon, walked the six blocks to the house, saw the live turkey, and went completely nuts. She started yelling out words I shall not repeat. She chained smoked and paced back and forth across the porch, mad as a hornet.

When Daddy arrived and saw his fine deal walking around on two feet, squawking and strutting, his eyes got big and round. Of course, being Daddy, he showed no surprise and remarked: "Looks like a real fine bird, Edith. Yes, sir, a real fine turkey."

Our father did not cook, clean house, or kill turkeys. That was woman's work. He did, however, shove aside the table and chairs so the basement door could be opened. During this, Mom glared at Daddy as if she'd like to wring his neck. Mom was steaming up like a locomotive. She grabbed the rope around the turkey's neck and proceeded to drag him down the steps into the dark dungeon to his ultimate fate: the axe.

As for Tom Turkey, who was not born yesterday, he began to sense all was not well. He somehow managed to break free and began running around and around the furnace. Mom was hot on this trail, wielding the axe like a seasoned storm trooper. Every time Mom got close to Tom, she'd take a mighty whack at him. Genie was right: feathers were flying like autumn leaves caught up by a sudden gust of wind. Genie and I were busy picking up feathers and trying to stay out of harm's way.

Mom was on one gigantic tear; there was no stopping her. In truth, Mom ran that turkey to death. When he finally collapsed and fell to the floor, gasping his final breath, the axe fell, and he lost his head. Blood was everywhere, and Genie and I had to clean it up.

After Tom Turkey was washed, plucked, stuffed, and roasted, I simply couldn't eat him, but Genie could. He ate both drumsticks with gusto.

Now looking down at my bloodstained coat, I not only remembered Tom Turkey, but I also thought of Big Red, as well. Life could get real sticky at times, that's for sure.

I got home late, just as Genie was coming in from basketball practice. He took one look at my face and his eyes glazed over; he looked so strange. "What happened to your face, Janny?" Genie's voice was no longer his brotherly voice; it was my Captain speaking to me. Not able to hold back my feelings, I sobbed out the whole sordid tale of the bully.

"Why didn't you tell me sooner?"

"I don't know . . . " my voice trailed off as more tears came rushing forth. Genie was pacing the floor and seemed to be talking to himself. Finally, he put his arm around me and told me to stop crying, for he would take care of it.

"What are you going to do, Genie?"

Genie looked over at me and coolly replied, "I'm going to kill the little bastard." That night, when the Super Chief came barreling through and our beds came together in the middle of the floor, Genie announced, "I've got a plan."

As usual, this came to no surprise to me; Genie always had "Plan A" and a backup "Plan B," and one called "AD," standing for Acute Desperation, to be used in extremes situations, and only when Plans A and B had failed. I didn't sleep a wink, but Genie slept like a log.

The following morning, I did exactly as I had been briefed. The plan was for me to do the same thing I always did, taking the same route home and acting normally, which was a big joke, as my heart was stuck in my throat. At the end of the day, I started for home. After several blocks, the bully fell in behind me. His first stinger caught me behind my ear, and oh, did it hurt! Tears sprang to my eyes, but I kept on walking. I was to walk fast but not run until I came to the spot Genie had mapped out for me.

The bully kept up his barrage of icy cold stingers, most of which found their mark. At last, I was at the spot where Genie had told me to break in to a dead run, and I did. I was looking wildly about for Genie, but I couldn't see him. The bully was nearly on me! His breath sounded like the Super Chief with a full head of steam. He was cursing, calling me names, and then he caught me by my pigtails and jerked my head back hard. I screamed, but my cries were drowned out by the most terrifying sound I'd ever heard.

It sounded like a cross between an animal in great pain and a car crash. The bully heard it, too, and let go of my hair. The screams grew louder and seemed to come out of nowhere, but this time I recognized the sound: it was the battle cry of Geronimo!

The bully and I turned around at the same moment. What I saw made my heart leap for joy. What the bully saw probably traumatized him for years to come; at least I hoped it did.

Genie came flying through the air, bare to the waist, his lean body covered in the red, yellow, black, and blue war paint of the Apache. Genie had the tomahawk he'd made in scouts strapped to his waist along with his hunting knife. Feathers, courtesy of Tom Turkey, were jutting out from his coal black hair in every direction. I knew for a fact (because Genie had read it to me) that the Apache warriors did not wear feathers: they wore cloth, usually red in color, tied about their heads.

But hey, the feathers looked great and added a whole lot of razzle-dazzle to the scene. Bedsides, I was sure the bully wouldn't know the difference. If he did, then he didn't have a moment to dwell on it. Genie leapt on the boy using his newly acquired jujitsu skills. He kicked the bully squarely in the chest, and the boy fell screaming in pain. Genie yelled louder, "So, you like to attack little girls, rub their faces in the snow, and bloody their noses?"

The bully hollered, "No, no!"

Genie shouted, "I see! On top of being a bully, you're also a liar!" Before the bully could say anything, Genie flipped him over onto his belly, sat down on his back, grabbed his head, and shoved it down hard beneath the snow. Each time the kid came up for air, Genie shoved him down again. After several minutes, the snow was awash in the color red.

The bully was screaming, "You broke my nose, and I'm telling my Dad. My Dad's a cop!"

"Good, kid," Genie said, "run home and get him. Hell, bring the whole damned police force. I'll show your Dad Janny's messed up face and her bloody coat. Then he can see and hear what bullies like you enjoy doing to little girls half their size and age who can't fight back."

The bully, now reduced to a whimpering puppy and shaking like a leaf, got to his feet. Genie grabbed him by his coat collar and spun him around to face him.

"Look at me, you sorry excuse for a human being, and get this message into your pea sized brain: If you or any of your buddies ever so much as look cross-eyed at my sister, then I'll come after you, rip your face off, tie your worthless butt to that track over there and wait for the Super Chief to grind you up into bite sized pieces. Understand?"

The bully managed to blubber out a weak, "Yes," while nodding his head up and down. When Genie let loose of him, he ran as if shot out of a cannon.

Walking home with Genie's arm around me, it began to snow. "Genie, I mean, Geronimo, aren't you cold?"

"Apache no feel cold, pain, fire, or bullet. Apache strong hombre." We both began to laugh, but I knew from this day until the end of my all my days that I'd never forget seeing the great Apache warrior flying through the air to rescue me, screaming out his war cry for God himself to hear.

When we got home, Genie washed both our faces and applied Mom's miracle Mercurochrome to every area needing tending. I made us a cup of Hershey's cocoa, giving Genie the last marshmallow in the package. Later, he brought his homework to the kitchen table and talked to me while I made dinner. He asked me about school. I didn't want to tell him how much school terrified me, so I said school was okay but I really missed being on the farm.

Genie smiled, "Summer will be here before you know it, sis, and we'll be back at our posts, taking care of the folks, and watching out for Nazis and Japanese Zeros. In the meantime, I don't think you'll have any more trouble with bullies, and I doubt very much if he brings his father—the cop—anywhere near us."

"You were a great Geronimo, Genie, the best."

"Think so?"

"Yeah, I know so." He smiled and finished his cocoa.

At 6 o'clock on the dot, Mom and Dad walked through the front door, stopped to wash their hands, and then sat down at the dinner table. I had made fried pork chops, potatoes, onions, milk gravy, string beans, biscuits, and iced tea. Three hundred and sixty-five days a year, my family drank iced tea and ate biscuits with every meal.

All during dinner, Genie and I waited for either parent to ask what happened to my face. Between us, we had made up a pretty good story, but we didn't need it: our parents didn't ask us any questions because they hadn't noticed my injuries.

How could this be? Our parents were overworked, underpaid, and lived on the edge of disaster and despair. What mattered to them that evening and every one following was the fact Genie and I were home, safe, supper was on the table, no one was crying, or missing, and one more day had somehow been gotten through. Daddy left for his second job, and Mom went to bed with her ever-present sinus headache.

Genie, wise beyond his years, not only understood the situation but also accepted it. He told me our folks were doing the best they knew how. I didn't understand grownups and did not always feel safe or loved, except by Genie. How many kids, if any, could say that the great warrior Geronimo had rescued them? I slept well that night, and all my dreams were happy ones.

The following Monday at school, everyone was talking about me and my big brother who was a full-blooded Indian who killed white boys on sight should they dare look at or mess with his sister, Janet Hall.

Needless to say, no more bullies attacked me, no more stingers were thrown, and no one pulled my hair, or called me names. The kids left me alone, which suited me just fine.

Genie had promised that summer was on its way. I could hardly wait to get back to the farm where I truly belonged. After all, we still had a war to win, a farm to protect, and Grandparents to love. For once, life didn't seem so hard, and I was feeling pretty darned good about everything.

Chapter Ten:

My Cow Reddy

Daddy continued working every spare job he could find. Mom, worn out and spirit-weary, had no time for fun or foolishness, as she put it. Her daily proclamation never changed. Every time I made a request, no matter how small, her reply was, "I've got supper to cook and chores to get done before my next shift. Life is hard, Janny. Times are hard. The sooner to you learn this fact, the better. You need to grow up. Now, peel the potatoes for supper, and I don't want to hear anymore about what you want."

When I felt I couldn't stand things the way they were for one more minute, I'd complain to Genie about Mom and her never-ending proclamations. Genie would sigh, put on his serious, grownup face, and take me by the hand to somewhere quiet. I didn't mind these serious talks because Genie would share things with me I didn't know about our family. He told me when he was a boy, Mom was patient and soft-spoken. She read him stories every night, helped him learn his times tables, and always encouraged him to stand up for himself when he thought he was right, and be a good listener when he was wrong.

He told me about the time he was invited with a group of boys from his class to the home of a wealthy family and he was nervous about going. He said Mom told him if their table was set with a lot of extra silverware and glassware, then he was to watch the hostess and do exactly as she did. Genie said that he watched his hostess like a hawk; whatever spoon she picked up, a split second later, he picked up the same spoon. This worked like a charm, and when he left, the hostess said, "Young man, you have excellent table manners."

Genie said he never forgot Mom's advice. He told me Mom loved a good joke and laughed a lot. Genie loved Mom, and I loved him for sharing her with me in this way. I guess when hard times come and don't leave, folks are bound to change.

My memories of our Mom were much different. Except for my Grandparents, the world of adults seemed to me to be a foreign land, uncomfortable, and at times, frightening. For the most part, I tried to steer clear of adults.

From the beginning, my heart belonged to those 40 ramshackle acres, as surely as the color blue belongs to the sky. Hard times or no, the farm offered Genie and me space and unstructured time to be children. While Genie learned the farming business inside and out, Grandma was teaching me to be a keen observer of the natural world. She demanded I give respect to any of God's creatures I encountered, including the two-legged ones.

Under her watchful, caring eyes, I read "Peter Pan," "Black Beauty," "Uncle Remus," many works of Mark Twain, and book after book of poetry. Poetry, she told me, should always be committed to memory whenever possible.

At night, lying beneath her handmade quilts and angel-embroidered pillowcases, gazing out of the window into the stars, I felt safe and snug in this land of Counterpane, where make-believe was real and often, dreams came true.

The farm was a living, breathing, and ever-changing wonder of wonders. It was alive and growing, and Genie and I were growing right along with it. I loved caring for the animals. Unlike humans, animals do not lie: they don't know how; they simply remain true to their nature. Many times, I thought I heard the animals talking amongst themselves. When I asked my Grandma about this, she'd laugh and say, "Of course they talk to one another. I love listening to my chickens talk."

"Grandma, what do your chickens talk about?"

She laughed, her eyes twinkling, "Why child, they say the same things you and Genie say: 'What's for supper?' "

I didn't care about hard times. All I knew was I never wanted to leave the farm. Genie had a million dreams; I had no other dreams because I was living mine.

It was clear to me, though I hated to admit it: Genie's time on the farm was a great train ride, a fabulous adventure, but it was not his final destination. Genie was someone who would go to the ends of the earth in search of his dreams. Deep inside my heart, I knew he would leave someday. The thought of his leaving made me want to die.

I've said Genie knew everything about everything, but more important was his ability, at a very early age, to take care of himself, me, and the world around him. Never in those childhood years did I hear anyone who knew him refer to Genie as a "little boy"; he was referred to as the "little man."

As for me, away from the farm, or away from Genie, my world was filled with giants, and I was always afraid. No matter how hard I tried to stop time or to slow it down, I could see and feel our childhood Shangri-La slipping away, and I was holding on for dear life. But life has one sure way of causing a child to let go. Life accomplishes this with a single blow to the heart: life introduces death.

In my brief twelve years of life, I had experienced what I called my "Gone to Heaven" stories. The loss of baby kittens, birds, rabbits, turtles, and goldfish were all mixed up with angels, prayers, lilacs, and wee graves marked with tiny crosses made from twigs. To each grave was added my letter of introduction to God on behalf of the dearly departed. It was all so lovely, not sad or dark as you might think, until the summer when death came suddenly, entering the sacred realm of childhood and changing me forever.

I suppose to adults the death of a cow is simply the death of a cow. But if the cow is someone you love and who loves you back, then everything in your world turns upside down.

Reddy was my cow, and along with Genie, my best friend. She was beautiful, kind, friendly of nature, and she kept all my secrets in the depths of her great, big blue-black eyes. Reddy loved me without knowing or caring why, and I loved her the same. She was small, standing barely 50 inches high (while the normal height for most cows was 61 to 65 inches, depending on the breed.)

We had three cows on our farm. Genie's cow was a large, gentle Guernsey the color of caramel. Genie named her Buttercup. She came from the island of Guernsey in the English Channel, and her milk was so rich, it had a golden tint.

Grandpa's cow was the largest, a big, black and white Jersey whose milk was high in butterfat, making it first choice by Meadow Gold Ice Cream Company and by Calico cat and her kittens. She came from northern Holland and had papers to prove it. Grandpa said that there was but one name for her, Queenie.

And then there was Reddy. No one had any idea where she came from or her breed. Reddy was a misfit, a runt who had been thrown in to sweeten the deal for the other two cows. Grandpa knew I'd love her. The first time I laid eyes on Reddy and she laid eyes on me, we connected. The two other cows stepped down the truck ramp and into our barnyard, but Reddy hesitated, until she looked at me, then pretty as you please, she walked down the ramp and headed straight for me. She stopped and stood, staring at me with those huge, velvet eyes. You could lose yourself in those eyes, and your heart, too, surely I did.

Cows are marvelous beings who act in direct regards to how they are treated. Cows are not dumb: they feel love and they feel pain. Cows enjoy being groomed and scratched behind the ears, chin, neck, and at the base of their tail. They like music—if it's not too loud, and they love being talked to. Grandma said a loved cow would give more milk and be a better mother to her calf.

Cows like living with other cows, and they become sad if they are left alone. If this happens, then they will try to form a bond of friendship with another animal, even something as small as a kitten. If no other animal is available, then they will bond with whatever they can find. Grandma told us a story about a neighbor's cow that fell in love with a pear tree. Every day after the milking, the cow would rush to the pear tree, rub against it, talk to it, rest beneath it, and never once ate its fruit or blossoms. When the cow died, the farmer and his wife buried her under the pear tree.

Genie thought the story was farfetched, but I loved it. Our cows loved to eat clover, wildflowers, and cherry blossoms should any blow their way. Cows have a great sense of smell. If Grandma made me blueberry pancakes, then Reddy would lick my face with her wide, coarse tongue. If I had eaten plain pancakes, then no licks were forthcoming.

Being creatures of habit, cows tend to follow the same path every day, kind of like humans. There is, of course, the exception to the rule, and that's where my story about Reddy really begins.

On a perfect Indian summer's day, Reddy, for reasons known only to her, decided to change her path. I can only suppose it was her nose that led her to the soybean field. I am quite sure Reddy had never seen soybeans growing, but she had tasted them in a mixture of other grains. Reddy must have decided she simply had to have another taste of those soybeans.

The fence surrounding the soybean field offered little resistance to her solid body. She merely leaned on the fence until it gave way then stepped lightly over it and into the biggest mistake of her so far gentle and uneventful life.

Genie and I knew something was wrong when Reddy didn't show up for milking. Buttercup and Queenie were standing at the barn door, mooing softly. Cows want to be milked, and it is painful for them to have to wait. Grandpa said he would milk both cows and for us to go and find Reddy. Since the soybean field was close by, we decided to look there first. Sure enough, there stood Reddy, shoulder high in soybeans and looking a bit sheepish, but otherwise alright. Genie put the fence right while I led Reddy back to the barn. I didn't have the heart to scold her.

After the milking, we went to supper to enjoy Grandma's fried chicken, biscuits, and gravy. After supper, Genie and I went back to check on Reddy. When we saw her, I screamed and gasped, "Oh, my God!"

Reddy had begun to swell up like a balloon. She looked as if she might burst! I had never seen anything like this, and I was terrified and began crying. Reddy saw me and walked slowly towards me, mooing pitifully. The other cows were kept in their stalls by a makeshift rope gate, but I'd never had to use one on Reddy; she liked her fresh hay and cool, clean water and never ventured out. She nuzzled my face with her own. Her usually wet nose was dry and hot.

"Genie," I cried, "come over here, quick! Something's terrible wrong with Reddy—" I couldn't finish. I threw my arms around her neck and sobbed.

"Janny, get a hold of yourself, soldier: you might scare Reddy."

I wiped my eyes, kissed Reddy's cheek, and tried so hard to be brave. I prayed Genie would know what to do: "I don't know what's wrong with Reddy, but I'm pretty sure it has something to do with her eating those damned soybeans," he said. "You had better run to the house and get Grandpa, on the double!"

I was running and crying and met Grandpa as he was coming out the back door. Somehow, in between my blubbers and tears, I told him what was happening to Reddy. "I was just coming down there to check on her myself. Now, you stop crying, honey," he said, his voice unusually soft. He wiped my face with his big, red bandanna and took hold of my hand.

Once inside the barn, I watched his face as he examined Reddy. He looked worried but didn't say a word. Then he mixed up some awful smelling green stuff and poured it down her throat. Reddy mooed loudly and began to switch her tail in a kind of frenzied motion as the green stuff gushed sickeningly out her nose. After three more ghastly attempts, Grandpa decided to call the veterinarian, Conrad Nelson.

Conrad was a distant cousin on Grandpa's side of the family. Everyone thought well of him. If someone couldn't pay their bill, then Conrad would readily accept eggs, an apple cobbler, roasting ears of corn, ham, a chicken, or pretty much whatever was offered, and always in a gracious manner.

When he took his first look at Reddy, his face fell. He told Grandpa, "Clyde, get the youngsters out of here." I heard him say in a much lower tone, "Is this Janny's cow?" Grandpa nodded that she was mine.

Conrad shook his head and murmured, "Well, it's a shame, Clyde, a real God-awful shame." Hearing those words drove fear and anguish even deeper into my heart.

Genie had hold of my hand and was walking towards the door but I broke free, running to Grandpa, screaming, "Please! Please, Grandpa, let me stay! Reddy needs me!" I was pleading, totally frightened half out of my mind. My heart was pounding so hard I thought I'd die. I saw Reddy looking over at me, her enormous eyes fastened to my face. I couldn't look away. Reddy was scared, too. How could she understand what was happening to her or why?

Grandpa's voice boomed, "Genie, get Janny up to the house, now!" Still crying and begging to stay, Genie literally dragged me out the door. I couldn't believe my Captain had not stood up for me, but I should have known better. When we were half way across the barnyard, Genie stopped, squeezed my hand, and whispered, "Stop crying, soldier, and follow me."

"Yes, Sir, Captain Sir," I sobbed. Of course my Captain had a plan—didn't he always? My heart leapt for joy. His plan was simple: we would climb the ladder that led to the hayloft and find a spot directly over Reddy's stall.

Genie removed some of the hay, smoothing out a neat bed for us to lie down upon. So far, neither Grandpa nor Conrad had heard anything. We settled ourselves on our stomachs. From our vantage point, we could see and hear everything going on below us. Genie gave me his military signal for keeping silent.

Dear, sweet Reddy was getting bigger. Her short legs looked as if they could no longer continue to hold her up. Her breathing was labored and came in short gasps, which matched the heaving of her sides. Her tail was limp and gray bubbles were forming about her nose. Conrad continued to pour bottle after bottle of dark, repulsive smelling liquid down Reddy's throat. But no sooner was the bottle was emptied then it would come right back up through her nose and out her bottom.

Reddy was a modest little soul and was mortified at what was being done to her. She began to groan and roll her eyes. Those soulful groans tore my very heart out. I had never heard sounds such as that before: I didn't know cows could cry in this way. She was wretched and crying for help. Reddy was in terrible, terrible trouble.

No longer able to stop the tears, I buried my face in Genie's soft, blue-flannelled shoulder. When I dared look again, I shook with horror: Conrad had taken out the longest hypodermic needle either Genie or I had ever seen. He began to plunge the needle slowly across Reddy's backside. Each time he drew the needle out, it left a hole the size of a silver dollar. It was a devastating sight to witness.

Reddy began to sway back and forth, her head down, her beautiful, silky neck stiff with brown slime. Reddy was hurting and everyone in the barn was hurting for her.

We heard Conrad explaining to Grandpa each and every soybean Reddy had eaten had swelled up double and triple their size in Reddy's stomach. Her stomach was full of gas and the holes were to relieve some of the pressure building inside of her . . .the only problem was the treatment wasn't working.

Hours passed. We had not taken our eyes off of Reddy. I was drowning in silent tears. My eyes, like my heart, were heavy, sinking into a deep, dark place. I was doing everything to keep from falling asleep, but I could feel myself slipping into exhaustion. Genie's hand rested on my head. How I longed to reach Reddy's head, to touch her and let her know I was there for her.

Genie was deathly quiet, staying strong for the two of us. Finally, my eyes closed and sleep smothered me in spite of my inner protests.

Around midnight, I felt Genie gently shaking me awake. His face was ashen in the moonlight. I looked down into Reddy's stall. She wasn't standing: she was lying down on her side, grossly swollen and not moving. My heart shattered instantly. Genie helped me down the ladder. I ran to Reddy's side and wrapped my arms around her neck. She was cold. Those lovely dark eyes were closed; her movie star, incredibly long lashes fanned her cheeks. I pressed my face against hers. Reddy had always smelled like a day-old puppy, which everyone knows is one of the sweetest scents on earth. Now she smelled of death. I was inconsolable. I kept telling Reddy I was there, that I loved her, and I prayed that somehow, in some way, she would know what she meant to me.

At some point, I heard Genie say he was going up to the house to get Grandpa. In a few minutes, they were back. I could see them standing beneath the lantern next to Queenie's stall. They were speaking in low, hurried voices.

As they spoke, it seemed I was entering a dark place, for inside the heart of every child exists a pitch-black, solemn place where light never enters. This is the place of screams, of cursed bits of unseen and unknown terror that linger, locked inside this chamber, waiting to be released by something horrendous, something unspeakable. When the horror comes, the chamber doors are flung wide and screams trample one another in their race to get free. Once out, they leave the child trembling in their wake. My door flew open because I suddenly remembered what farmers did with their dead animals.

Genie and Grandpa were staring at me, and then Genie was holding me, for he, too, remembered. "Genie, Genie," I sobbed, "Don't let Grandpa sell Reddy to the glue factory. Please, Genie, please."

Genie and I knew about the glue factory. We had seen it for ourselves. We had seen the steel hammer of death, the sharp knives that sliced skin from bone in strong, even strokes. We had seen the vats of grisly, gruesome muck that turned once beautiful and graceful creatures into gray sludge and finally, into neat little bottles of pristine white paste.

In kindergarten and on into first grade, I had been a devoted paste-eater. I loved eating paste: it tasted like peppermint. *Dear God!* I thought, feeling sick, *How many Reddy's had I already eaten?*

I began to throw up, falling face down in the hay next to Reddy. If they came for Reddy's body, then they could take me, too. My mind was made up.

In the lantern light, I could see Genie's face, and I knew he was pleading my case, mine and Reddy's. I understood hard times: it was the one thing I did know. I knew a dead cow could bring as much as $50, and I knew Grandpa needed every dime he could get, but it didn't matter. I was not going to give up Reddy for Grandpa, for God, and especially not for money.

I hated the word *money*. All my life, thus far, had been constantly fraught with questions about money: Where would we get money? When was the money coming? Was there enough money? It had been stamped into my brain to the point of forcing out every little daydream I ever had. Life, to me, seemed horribly unfair. But fair or not, I didn't care: I was not connected to the world, but I was connected to Reddy.

After what seemed a thousand eternities, Genie came over and sat down beside me in the hay. He put his arms around me and said softly, "Don't cry, Janny. Everything's okay. Grandpa is not going to sell Reddy to the glue factory. I'm going to plow Lester Bocock's extra field of rye and give the money to Grandpa. It will be about the same as what he'd get for Reddy."

I was so overcome with feelings of love and gratitude I couldn't speak. I buried my head in Genie's chest and squeezed his hand once; he squeezed back twice, as was our custom.

Genie and I heard a lot about adults having lived longer and having had more life experience. I had to admit this was true, but I can tell you for sure: adults don't have the corner on feelings. Children's hearts have the ability to feel as much as any adult, and in some cases, they feel more.

Genie told me to prepare a large pail of warm, soapy water to clean Reddy for her burial while he went to the tool shed to gather up every heavy chain he could find.

I washed Reddy from head to hoof, toweled her dry, and gently brushed her still soft body. As I worked, I suddenly remembered the bunches of lavender Grandma had hung in the pantry to dry. I ran to the house to get some, stopping to look in Grandma's ribbon box and finding exactly what I wanted. Back in the barn, I tied a lovely purple satin ribbon intertwined with sprigs of lavender around Reddy's neck. She looked like a princess, and she smelled heavenly.

When Genie came into the barn with the chains, he looked at Reddy and then at me. He touched my head and murmured, "Good job, Janny. Good job."

Genie went straight to work, fastening the chains around Reddy's feet. Then he backed up the old Allis Chalmers tractor to the barn door, hooked Reddy's chains to the back of the tractor and fired it up. He began to pull Reddy, slowly, still on her side, out of the door into the barnyard, and down the grass road leading to the cornfield. The moon was high. I loved moonlight and thought it a fitting atmosphere as I walked next to my friend. It was a strange funeral procession: a skinny boy on a tractor pulling a very stiff, swollen cow, followed by a weeping girl, a white duck, and a barking dog bringing up the rear. Nevertheless, we were a sincere, truehearted funeral procession, determined to give Reddy her due, a proper sendoff attended by those who knew and loved her. I wanted Buttercup and Queenie to be there, but Genie said he didn't think we could manage it, and it wouldn't do to have the guests wandering off into the cornfield.

Finally, we arrived at the place Genie had chosen. Although it was still Indian summer and we had not had the first frost, the ground was a whole lot harder than it should have been. Genie had to use a pickaxe to soften the earth for digging, and dig we did, shoveling dirt to the point of exhaustion, but we didn't give up. When I was able to stand up straight in the hole, we knew the grave was deep enough, but to our mutual dismay, not wide enough. Reddy was a small cow, but a cow, nonetheless. So, back to work we went. I could feel the blisters forming on the palms of my hands. And I knew Genie's were worse, as he was able to work twice as hard.

Just when I thought I could not lift one more shovel of dirt, Grandpa arrived on the scene carrying a thermos of hot chocolate and bacon and egg sandwiches. While we ate and drank, Grandpa took a turn with the shovel and finished out the sides of Reddy's grave. He climbed out of the grave, smiled at our tired, sad faces, and murmured something that sounded like, "Never in my born days . . ." then he left.

The sun was soon to be up when we lowered Reddy into her final resting place. I have to say that lowering her in was a kind of push and shove job, but we managed. As we were covering up the grave, I looked out over the field of corn, which had long since been harvested, and I noticed the corn stalks were bent over from the middle, or from the waist, if you will. To me, they looked like a congregation bowed in prayer. I pulled on Genie's shirtsleeve, directing him to look at the corn field.

Genie enjoyed a healthy imagination, but he was a warrior; however, he was well aware of my penchant for fanciful reveries, and he instinctively knew what I was thinking: "You think those corn stalks look as if they might be praying, don't you Janny?"

I nodded my head firmly and did not feel even a little foolish. For several minutes, Genie didn't say a word. He stood looking out over the cornfield, and then he looked at me for a long time and then at Reddy's grave. Genie was a thinker, a doer, and not often prone to my imagination's kind of peculiarities. But above all, and you can ask anyone who ever knew him, Genie was a fair-minded person. He walked over to me and placed his hand on my head. My braids had long since come undone, and I felt his fingers straightening out the waves. I knew he had been weighing his heart against his mind and had decided, without a doubt, the heart had won.

Genie had brought his Bible along, but I didn't need it. I recited the 23rd Psalm from memory. I knew God would welcome Reddy; after all, He created her.

On the ride back to the barn, I stood behind Genie on a slim piece of iron welded beneath the tractor seat, mere inches from the ground. Falling off never occurred to me, for it was matter of trust in my Captain.

Reddy's death had propelled me forward into the world of adults. Mom was forever talking about how everything in life is part of the "big plan." I had no idea what she meant, but it worried and scared me. I started to cry.

All at once, without so much as a hum or a whistle, Genie started to sing. You guessed it, another Johnny Mercer tune. He sand loud and clear in the silvery moonlight:

> Glow, little glow-worm, fly of fire,
>
> Glow like an incandescent wire,
>
> Glow for the female of the specie,
>
> Turn on the A-C and the D-C;
>
> This night could use a little brightnin',
>
> Light up, you li'l ol' bug of lightnin',
>
> When you gotta glow, you gotta glow,
>
> Glow, little glow-worm, glow . . . .

His song dried my tears, and I said, "Genie, you are a natural born great singer."

"Hell, sis, I'm a natural born phenomenon," he laughed. Phenomenon was another word Genie had taught me.

We sang, laughed, and looked up at the big, beautiful, fading moon surrounded by a jillion stars, and I wondered if God had somehow made Genie to be my brother and fitted him into my "big plan." Whatever answers I didn't know didn't matter, not on this night. I was glad Genie was my brother, my Captain, and my best friend.

But I remember the first time I saw Genie as more than my big brother. It was towards the end of the school year. Genie had been elected as the new president of the Hi-Y Association, which was part of the YMCA. He was to give a speech in front of the whole school, faculty, board members of the YMCA, and local officials.

My folks were not there; they never came to the high school for any event. I think it hurt Genie's feelings, but he never spoke about it. I was not allowed to leave the house after school, but I broke the rules and went to hear Genie. I slipped into the back door of the auditorium; the entire place was standing room only. I stood in front of one of the marble columns.

When I saw Genie walking up the aisle, my heart sank. Genie didn't own a sports jacket, let alone a suit. But there he was wearing a navy-blue blazer with brass buttons that was obviously two sizes too small. The jacket's sleeves didn't come anywhere near his wrists, and they could not cover up the frayed white cuffs of one of Daddy's old dress shirts. Genie looked ridiculous, like a 6'2" Charlie Chaplin! People around me were nodding and whispering. "This was the fellow the student body chose to be their president?" some kids were snickering.

If Genie saw or heard anything going on, he never let on. He strode up onto the stage, smiling, waving to his friends, and shaking hands with everyone on the stage. There was a natural grace about his walk and mannerisms. You would have thought he was attired in a thousand dollar Hickey Freeman suit from Muses Men's shop in downtown Atlanta.

After the invocation by the mayor, Genie stepped up center stage to the mike. My heart was breaking: he looked like a clown. He thanked everyone for coming and then said, "My name is Dewey E. Hall, and I have the serious honor to be the senior president of the Marion High School Hi-Y Club of Grant County, Indiana. As president, I've something important to say to you, but before I begin, and with your kind permission and generous understanding, I'd like to remove this sports coat, which was loaned to me by a friend. The problem is this coat is so tight, I can't move my arms high enough to take the notes of my speech out of my pocket."

For a moment, the audience was absolutely quiet, and then people suddenly responded by clapping, smiling, and chuckling respectfully. At this point, the principal got up and helped Genie off with the coat. Genie rolled up his sleeves and loosened his black funeral tie.

Genie called Daddy's black tie the Funeral Tie because the only time it was seen out of the closet was when somebody died.

Genie flashed his irresistible smile, those black shoe-button eyes shining, fastening on every face seated before him. His voice reached every ear to the very back of the auditorium, filling everyone present with warmth, sincerity, and honest to goodness know-how far beyond his 17 years.

I saw power for the first time being used in a way I was not familiar with, and it was amazing. This was a Genie I didn't know existed.

The next thing I knew, I was hearing the clapping, the cheers, and the bravos. I don't know what he talked about, but I knew he was a winner. I looked up at the stage and watched people shaking Genie's hand, congratulating him. He was standing tall, a darn good-looking fellow, this Dewey E. Hall. I knew I'd never forget this moment, this grand showcase of the man my brother was to become, but even amidst the cheering crowd, I had my own favorite memory of this fellow: Genie standing knee deep in the black dirt of an Indiana cornfield, at midnight under a full moon, delivering a eulogy fit for any monarch or president, a eulogy for a dead cow, my cow, Reddy.

Chapter Eleven:
The Second Star to the Right . . .

Like most children, I wholeheartedly believed in magic, especially the magic of wishes. After all, Peter Pan believed in them: he was living proof. Even Genie, who knew everything about everything, was quick to give Peter Pan his due.

"A great fighter, he'd be a fine lad for our Army. You never know, Janny, when we see one of those shooting stars, it might just be Pan catching a ride home for supper."

"Where does Peter Pan live, Genie, I mean for real?"

"You mean beyond his own special 'second start to the right and straight on til morning'?"

"Yes."

"Well, I'm not entirely 100% sure, but I'd have to say that Peter has his own world of glittering stars hidden deep inside our universe, a place where 'wishing stars' never die, as long as there are children who need them. These stars will shine beyond all the forevers . . . ."

I believed Genie's every word. It was clear to me: no child could live long in a world without wishes and imagination.

So far my daily experiences registered first with my heart, then with my head. As a result, my feet were well off the beaten path and my head lost in the clouds. So far, my time in Genie's army had done nothing to change my firm belief that imagination was everything; imagination was as necessary to me as candles on a stormy night.

I had to admit Genie was a freethinker, but I noticed whenever I was standing at the bedroom window late at night, watching for shooting stars to wish on, he'd be standing right beside me, ready to send forth his wish. Most of my wishes didn't come true. Once, I asked Genie, "Why?"

His answer was, "Look here, Janny, millions of kids like us, all over the world, are making wishes, too. You have to take turns."

"With a million other kids?"

"Sure."

I didn't like his answer, but I accepted it; after all, Genie knew everything about everything. He believed in answering all questions put to him, and he hated it when adults wouldn't give him an answer.

Wishes and dreams were a big part of my life. Genie's life was the War, the farm, school, sports, and me, followed by the world. Sometimes life got pretty hard and difficult to understand. Something bad was happening all around us, and Genie said, "Something's not right, sis. We need to find out what's going on."

For some time, Genie and I had overheard the adults talking in low tones and using strange, unfamiliar words, words like *Parkinson's*, *progressive*, *rigidity*, *tremors*, *Blufton Clinic*, *terminal*, *deterioration*, and *inanition*, which caused Genie to race to Grandma's old, tattered, green Webster to look up its meaning. He was supposed to tell me what he found out but instead he put me off, saying, "Janny, there is plenty of time for you to know about such things."

The words *such things* frightened me because they were the words grownups frequently used when they did not intend to tell you anything. I couldn't believe Genie was using those words with me. I felt scared, even sad, but sad about what? If Genie knew, then he wasn't telling me—this time.

The answer to my questions came together in one brief moment, in an instant that seemed so insignificant.

On a particularly crisp October morning, everything appeared normal in my Grandma' cozy kitchen: she was standing at the stove making my favorite breakfast: two large, brown eggs with yolks broken, flattened, fried flat as a pancake, and tough as shoe leather. I preferred this breakfast above all others.

I was perched atop the butter churn, reciting my favorite poem, Longfellow's "The Wreck of the Hesperus." I had finally memorized all 22 verses. I could tell my Grandma was pleased. I had reached the eighteenth verse:

> She struck where the white and fleecy waves
>
> Looked soft as carded wool,
>
> But the cruel rocks, they gored her side
>
> Like the horns of an angry bull.

As I spoke the last word of the verse, Grandma called out to me—her voice sounded high and strange. All those scary feelings suddenly came together, and I was afraid. I jumped off of the butter churn and ran to her side, "Grandma? Grandma, what's wrong?"

I saw tears forming at the corners of her eyes; she was having trouble getting her words out, and she was staring at her hands. "Help me, Janny. Help me, child," she choked. I was crazed to help her, but I couldn't see what she needed me to do. What did she need help with?

My eyes followed hers downward to the skillet; the eggs were ready to be turned,
the spatula beneath them, but my Grandma was unable to make the simple wrist
movement necessary to turn the eggs over.

Shocked and terrified, I took the spatula from her hand, turned the eggs over, and removed the skillet off of the wood-burning stove. Then I took my Grandma's hand and slowly walked her to her chair. Her hands felt cold as ice, and her arms were stiff, especially her right one. When we got to the chair, she slumped down into it like a tired child. I was crying hard. I knew something terrible was happening. My beloved Rock of Gibraltar had just crumbled before my eyes. I needed Genie and Grandpa.

As soon as I had made her comfortable, spreading her sky-blue shawl around her shoulders, removing her shoes, and putting a pillow under her feet, I was out the back door and running fast. Spot joined me, barking loudly, sounding the only alarm he could.
When we reached the cornfield where they were plowing, they took one look at my wild eyes and tear-stained face and joined me in the run back to the house.

Grandma sat where I had left her; Grandpa rushed to her side, "Florrie, Florrie, it's Clyde. If you can, I want you to take hold of my hand."

But Grandma didn't move. Only her eyes moved: they met, searched his, and held. I was sobbing, tugging on Genie's arm. He looked down at me. He was crying, and Genie never cried.

Grandpa placed pillows on both sides of Grandma. His movements were gentle, and his big, sun browned, calloused hands were trembling. Grandma shut her eyes, and I gasped. Genie grabbed my hand and whispered, "It's okay, Janny. She's only fallen asleep."

Grandpa asked me to finish up the breakfast. I wasn't hungry, so I gave my eggs to Spot, who gobbled them up with pleasure. Genie and I wanted to be close to Grandma, so we sat down at her feet. After a little while, she opened her eyes and saw us there. In a halting voice, she asked me to finish the poem I had started.

I began, "Such was the wreck of the Hesperus, / in the midnight and snow . . ." but I couldn't say anymore. I was choking on my tears. I buried my head in her lap and heard Genie finish the poem: "Christ save us all from a death like this, / on the reef of Norman's woe."

Grandma tried to smile, tried to lay her hand on my head—both seemed to take an extreme effort, but she managed. Grandpa had pulled his old rocker up next to her chair. Looking in her eyes, it was easy to see she was glad the three of us were there with her.

After we helped put Grandma to bed, we went upstairs to our room. I was feeling sick to my stomach, so Genie went downstairs and brought me back a Coca-Cola and a handful of saltine crackers, which I ate between sobs.

"Where's Spot, Genie?" Spot always came upstairs with us and slept at the foot of the bed.

"He stayed downstairs with Grandma; he'll be along after awhile."

The Coca-Cola was helping to settle my stomach but not doing anything for the fear and dread filling my heart. I begged Genie to tell me what he had learned from the old Webster about the scary words we had heard.

Genie was an expert when it came to explaining a subject. He liked to interpret and was ever diligent in making sure I understood. But he wasn't saying a word and his silence frightened me.

"Genie," I pleaded, "you've just got to tell me what you know."

Genie got up slowly from the bed, walked across the room, and returned with a
candle. He lit the candle and placed it on the table next to his side of the bed. I sat up,
and in the soft glow of candlelight, Genie looked, for the entire world, like Peter Pan. This was strange because it wasn't the Genie I knew. Genie was Tarzan, the Lone Ranger, Geronimo, the Green Hornet, but never Peter Pan.

Peter Pan didn't want to grow up, while Genie couldn't wait to be a grown up. He had planned his whole life; he had places to go, things to see and do. He looked so different . . . . I was petrified. My happy secure world was tumbling down around me.

At last, Genie began to speak. His voice was low, his words measured. "The truth is, Janny, there is something terribly wrong going on inside of Grandma's body. It's been there a long, long time and it is slowly killing her . . .and there is nothing the doctors can do to stop it."

"But Grandma hasn't been to see a doctor."

"I'm afraid she has, while we were back in school. Grandpa took her to Blufton Clinic; they just never told us."

I couldn't hold back the tears and neither could Genie. We buried our faces in our pillows and cried until we could cry no longer. Old Spot heard us crying and came bounding up the stairs, leapt up onto the bed and began licking our faces frantically. He wouldn't quit licking until we stopped crying.

I've heard people say animals don't feel or show compassion like humans do, but I say they are dead wrong. Animals feel deeply; they know when someone they love is sick or in trouble.

Take old Spot for instance—Spot was a first-rate rabbit dog, probably the best there was in Grant County. Spot loved to hunt rabbits better than he loved to eat. When Dad would get the gun out of the closet, Spot would commence to dance abut on his hind legs, barking with joy, ready to go. But starting the next morning after the egg frying incident with Grandma, until the day she died, Spot never chased another rabbit. When the rifle came out of the closet, Spot would look up at Dad with sad eyes and whimper, and then go lie down next to Grandma's chair. Spot became a totally different dog. He devoted himself to Grandma, never leaving her side.

Spot changed from fearless hunter to gentle caretaker. He became quiet, patient about his mealtime, and somehow regal. He had appointed himself Grandma's Guardian Angel. He understood she could not lift her hand to touch him, so he would walk over and push his head up beneath her hand and there he would stand until he felt it was okay to lie down again.

That night was a turning point in our lives, a great huge "life lesson," one for which even Genie had not been prepared. As we stood at our window to the stars, they appeared, like always, twinkling in their awesome magic. All at once, we saw shooting stars, several at a time, darting out into the midnight blue.

Genie and I made two extremely heartfelt wishes, actually there were three if you counted Spot's, and of course, we did. After all, Spot had earned his right to wish on his shooting star; he knew what to wish for better than anyone.

Beloved Grandmother, Flora Belle Nelson

Beloved Grandfather, Clyde Guy Nelson

Chapter Twelve:

Even Angels Die

According to Mr. Webster or Mr. Oxford, "An angel is a person who performs a mission for God or acts as if sent by God. A person possessing inner beauty, purity, or kindness. One who puts others first." In short, the definition of angel was a perfect description of our Grandmother, Flora Belle Nelson.

Of course, she would not hear of herself being called an angel. She would say, "A good egg will suffice."

Grandma clearly understood what was happening to her in regards to the Parkinson's. Uppermost in her mind was her poignant desire not to be managed. She was keenly aware of the enormous effort it took for one tiny decision such as moving her finger. Genie and I sadly watched as her choices diminished on a daily basis. She observed this disintegration out the depths of her beautiful hazel eyes, eyes that spoke volumes while her lips remained silent.

One of the horrors of Parkinson's is it leaves part of the brain intact while, in a systematic fashion, it destroys the body's ability to perform the simplest of tasks, like walking, talking, eating, and swallowing. The thinking part of the brain knows exactly what is going on, leaving the eyes and the heart to record the destruction.

Friends came to visit and talked amongst themselves as if Grandma were not in the room or had suddenly gone deaf. Such treatment infuriated Grandma, but somehow she managed to keep her sense of humor. One afternoon, following a visit from a jolly group of whispering do-gooders, Grandma pointed to a book on the table Genie had been reading. I ran to fetch it for her, placing the book in her lap.

She pointed to the title—*The Invisible Man*—then she pointed to herself. We laughed.

Grandma continued to enjoy listening to the radio. She loved Jack Benny, Fibber McGee and Molly, Amos and Andy, and especially Senator Cleghorn of Allen's Alley. Sunday, since she could no longer attend church, was reserved for hours of the evangelist of the day. Grandma loved hearing The Word. This was the time when Genie and I would carry out our military duties. We made the rounds of all the checkpoints and kept a sharp eye for unusual activity. We gave messages for our animal corps to deliver, studied maps, and continually watched the night sky for signs of Nazi paratroopers.

Genie said, "If those bastards land in our cornfield and break a leg, I'll shoot the son-of-a-bitches where they fall." Genie was a lot angrier these days, and I was a lot sadder. Genie was angry because he couldn't help Grandma get better. He was one of those people who were awfully good at solving life's problems, but he couldn't solve this one.

I missed my Grandma's giant hugs. She was made of marshmallow softness with no sharp edges. Most grownups I knew had sharp edges. Grandma smelled of lilacs, gingerbread, and hot chocolate on a winter's day. The thing about her hugs were no matter how big or small you happened to be, you could walk into those outstretched arms and fit inside like a glove.

Whenever the doctor came, Genie and I would wait until Grandpa was serving him coffee and apple pie, then we'd sneak his black bag, take it into the parlor, and read everything concerning Grandma.

Genie, whose own penmanship resembled chicken scratches, had no trouble deciphering the doctor's remarks. We also eavesdropped whenever possible. What we learned shattered both our hearts: Grandma didn't have long to live. We weren't babies; we knew people died, but knowing didn't help when it was Grandma . . .when it was happening now . . . .

We still said our prayers at night, which were more like pleas, more like begging, than prayers. Grandma was rapidly following the pattern laid out by the disease. The doctor outlined this horrendous progression so Grandpa and the rest of us would know what to expect. Grandma was literally starving to death; she could no longer swallow the strawberry ice cream she loved so well. When Mom and Dad came, Mom wanted us to go back to town with them, but we set up such a fuss, they gave in and let us stay.

One afternoon, as I was sitting on Grandma's bed, she pointed to her feet, which were uncovered. They had taken on a decidedly bluish tint. When she noticed this, she pointed to the Sears catalogue which was also on the bed. Mom placed the catalogue on a pillow in front of her, and I slowly turned the pages.

It wasn't long before Mom and I realized Grandma was picking out a dress—the dress in which she would be buried. The dress she chose cost $12.98, and we could see the worry in her eyes. Mom told her the price was fine. The dress was navy-blue crepe with a white collar and cuffs; the skirt was accordion pleated. Mom later told me it was the first new dress Grandma had gotten since I had been born.

Grandma, early on, had said the funeral was to be held at Morris Chapel, where she was a charter member, having played the piano and taught Sunday school there for many years. Mom also had a keepsake box Grandma had given to her over a year ago. Inside the box were the instructions for her funeral.

She had three requests: she wanted three hymns played—"The Old, Rugged Cross," "It's Only One Step More," and "Rock of Ages." She asked for the 23rd Psalm, verses 4 through 6 to be read by Genie, if he felt he could, and her third and final request was to be buried in silk stockings, having never owned a pair in her lifetime.

Late one night, I went downstairs to the kitchen to get Genie and me another slice of chocolate cake and some milk. Grandma's sister, Nellie, was visiting at the time. As I was slicing the cake, I heard loud voices coming from the direction of the parlor. I went to investigate, but I was careful to keep out of sight. I peeked in and saw my Mother standing in front of the heavy mahogany table, which would soon hold our Grandmother's casket.

Mom and Nellie were having quite a row. Genie and I never liked Nellie much. She rarely visited Grandma, even after being told how ill she was. When she finally did come, she was full of "shoulds." Grandpa *should* have done this; Mom *should* have done that. She walked around the house as if it were hers. I never saw her hug Grandma, fix her pillows, or even press ice chips against her lips. I heard Nellie say, "In my opinion, Edith, I think cotton stockings will do nicely. After all, she'll be dead, so who's to know?"

That's when Mom exploded: "Damn you, Nellie, I'll know! I'm buying Mom the sheerest Belle Sharmers money can buy, and that's the end of it!"

Nellie looked down her nose at Mom and said in a smug voice, "You don't have any money, Edith."

"I'll get the money, Nellie, and if you ever mention this conversation to anyone, I'll slap you silly!"

Nellie didn't say a word. She stormed out of the room and never saw me standing there. I was so proud of my Mom for standing up to Nellie, as few people did. Genie was proud, too, when I told him.

Parkinson's had put our Grandmother through years of torture and pain, and had reduced this bright, active, loving lady to total helplessness. Yet, despite this tragedy, Grandma somehow retained her dignity. She would not let a mere disease define who she was or what she was worth. Genie said Grandma was nothing short of a hero. I agreed.

In the weeks following Nellie's visit, Genie and I spent all the time we could with Grandma, even missing some school days. Spot never left her side. Spot was a loving, attentive companion, who frequently licked Grandma's hands without a hint of embarrassment.

Genie and I kept Grandma's spirits up by relating the daily events taking place on the farm. When we told her Grandpa was searching for a replacement for the infamous Big Red, she cracked up. We could see the laughter dancing in her eyes. We lived for these brief moments when once again, our life was as it used to be, how we thought it would always be.

I reported to her every flower that bloomed and how our oldest sow had turned out to be a good mother, after all. Genie related the story of a baby barn owl that fell down the well screeching and flapping its wings to a fare-thee-well. He was white fluff and all beak but very smart. When Genie lowered the bucket down the well, the little fellow hopped right in and Genie pulled him up. Genie turned the bucket on its side on the ground; the owl walked to the edge of the rim, looked up at Genie's face, glanced at the stars and then at the barn, paused and took flight.

Grandma always told us, "Children, life doesn't always have happy endings, so be sure to celebrate grandly when it does."

Before she became sick, Grandma and I loved to take long walks. I remember once around Christmas time when were walking in the woods. A light snow was beginning to fall; soon the trees would look as if they were wrapped in ermine. Winter walks were special because of the stillness all around, no rustling of leaves or sounds of creatures scurrying here and yon. We talked in whispers, like in church. We were walking along the creek, parts of which were frozen with a thin sheet of ice. Suddenly, Grandma bent down and picked up a tiny brown sparrow. It lay on her blue mitten undamaged, asleep. She handed the frozen little body over to me.

"Grandma, did this sparrow starve to death?"

"Possibly, Janny, but it's my guess it became lost in last evening's snow storm, was forced from the sky by the wind, and died from exhaustion."

I was wiping my tears when we found several more. Grandma told me to make a place in the snow and cover them over with twigs and branches.

"Winter is hard on wee things, Grandma," I said sadly.

"Winter is hard on everyone but these plain little fellows, without much style or colorful plumage, do have something special."

"What? What do they have, Grandma? What makes them special?"

"I thought we talked about this last spring."

"No, Grandma, we didn't. Tell me now."

"Well, Janny girl, the things I'm about to tell you can't be proven, except by one's own heart. But I believe of all the beautiful birds the good Lord created, the lowly sparrow was his favorite. I believe this because Christ himself liked to be around plain folks, sometimes lowly-type folks. Sparrows are the plain folk of the bird kingdom. Sparrows abide, Janny. They simply abide."

Then she went on to hum the hymn "Abide with me": "When other helpers fail and comfort flee / Help of the helpless, O abide with me."

"Grandma?" I asked, "Am I one of God's favorites?" I knew Genie was a favorite because he was everybody's favorite.

Grandma looked at me, surprised, "Of course, you are, Janny; you're a hundred-percent favorite."

We came to the clearing located midway through our woods. It was one of Genie's most important outposts to watch for Nazis falling out of the sky. But on this morning, the clearing was filled with a flock of black crows, all talking at once and strutting about in their black, shiny slickers.

Grandma nudged my arm, "Who do you suppose is the leader of this crowd? Now don't you dare tell me they all look alike. Study each one: observe them as individuals."

This was Grandma 101. She and Genie delighted in giving me little life problems to solve, as she called them. I sat down on a log, and I watched. I studied, and finally, I came up with my choice. And a great choice it was, too. My guy was bigger than the others; he talked nonstop, had the loudest voice, and the best swagger. Yes, he was my man, my crow of choice. When I proudly pointed him out to my Grandmother, she smiled her special "adult smile." I recognized it immediately; it meant, "Sorry, you're wrong."

Sure enough, in the next few minutes, a small crow, one whom I hadn't even noticed, took flight. The flock rose in one body and took to the air behind him.

My guy was still strutting about, speaking volumes to an empty field. When he realized his flock had flown away without him, he panicked and raced around in a circle for a moment or two before flying upward to join them.

Grandma laughed, "Don't rush to judgment, Janny girl. You'll learn." Grandma put her arm around me, and we walked towards the house. I didn't always "get" Grandma's life lessons on the first go 'round, but one thing I knew for sure: I didn't know a darn thing about crows!

Later after supper, I told Genie about the crows. He laughed, "Hey, sis, don't worry: I've got a book on crows you can study."

I began to think Genie and Grandma were two of a kind. I really didn't want to study crows. Actually, sometimes I rather liked not knowing facts, then I could imagine or think whatever I pleased. But this would never do, not with Genie or Grandma. I hoped with everything going on Genie would forget about the book on crows, but I seriously doubted it because Genie loved to give me surprise quizzes. Like Grandma, he was a born teacher; it came as natural to him as his smile. But it's tough when you happen to be the only student.

To Genie's way of thinking, the glass was always half full, and by Heaven, it was his job to fill 'er up! Both Grandparents were optimists; Dad was a fighter who wouldn't give up or give in, and Mom was extremely practical with a bit of the fatalist thrown in, a kind of "whatever will be" attitude.

And then there was me. Genie, of course, knew he could straighten me right out. Dad had no comment, and Mom said, "You're not at all like your brother." But Grandma had me pegged, and she worried over me. She told me after one of our "life courses," "Janny, you want reality to be tied up with ribbons, and that's not how the world works."

Except for the farm, the world seemed to me to be occupied by giants, bullies, adults who never made time for you, Nazis falling out of the sky, and Japanese soldiers who everyone said ate little children. I figured the world could use a few ribbons.

Genie told me, "Janny, tie the ribbons in your hair," and handed me his book on crows. The honest-to-goodness truth was I couldn't face reality without the ribbons, and I was having a heap of trouble facing the fact our beloved Grandmother was dying.

We never left Grandma alone. To pass the time, we took turns reading to her until she drifted into sleep. One afternoon, I took the huge family Bible from its special place and began to look at it carefully. It was a beautifully ornate book with gold-tipped pages and heavenly pictures in lush colors, each picture covered with a very thin tissue to protect it. The beginning of each chapter was lettered in gold leaf, in elaborate scroll, especially the Psalms. There were also about twelve satin ribbons in brilliant colors to be used to mark your place. In between the pages were countless baby pictures, the deed to the farm, birth and death certificates, poems and drawings Genie and I had made for her and private letters, which I did not open. What surprised me was I found just two pressed flowers: a tiny bouquet of purple violets and a single sprig of lily-of-the-valley; beside it was written the name of my sister, Mary Anna Ella.

The yard around the house was home to hundreds of flowers. Grandma loved them so, but in her Bible, there were only the two. I decided I would ask her about this when she woke, but she never woke up fully. Her eyes would open and shut regularly, but she could no longer speak. Three days later, to the hour, as the doctors had predicted, our loving angel and best friend in the entire world, Flora Belle Nelson, died.

Paradise had ended. We knew we would never again experience this kind of magic. Genie said, "There would be many more trips to the stars, but trips beyond them, where we had been, came but once in a lifetime."

Genie found out and reported to me that our dear Grandmother was, indeed, wearing real silk Belle Sharmer hose—the best money could buy—when she was laid to rest.

The morning we left the farm, I took with me a handful of cherry blossoms, my collection of bird feathers, a shiny pebble from the creek, and a small bag of Indiana corn. I don't know what Genie took, and I didn't ask him. Some thing's are too close to the heart to speak of out loud.

Genie told me we were never coming back to the farm. Spot knew this, too, but he preferred not to hang around for the sad goodbyes. Spot knew we loved him and would understand his leaving.

As the hearse drove past Morris Chapel, I thought of Mary Anna Ella and noted the daffodils blooming in yellow splendor upon her grave. I glanced over at Genie and saw tears streaming down his face. I quickly turned away out of respect for my Captain, my compatriot, my partner in a childhood so powerful in its measure of love the memories would literally save my life in the years to come.

That raggedy old farm had fed our hearts, stimulated our minds, and comforted our souls for all those extraordinary summers, giving me a sense of place and belonging. The farm had given Genie the time and space to discover who he really was, what he could become, and how to turn dreams into reality.

Until the day I die, I know I will never forget the touch and smell of Reddy's warm flank against my cheek, the glorious wonder of the cherry orchard in full bloom, or the death of downy, wee things gone straight to Heaven without a peep; the heavenly scent of purple lilacs following an April rain, the taste of Grandma's fried chicken on a Sunday afternoon, Grandpa's big grin and booming laughter, Mama hens clucking softly to their chicks, or summer's incredibly blue skies overrun with cloud-pictures. I'd remember Pearl Circle's homemade black walnut ice cream, baby kittens sunning fat lil' tummies on the back porch, a field of corn knee-high on the Forth of July, and our Grandmother's voice reading the Bible after the house had gone to sleep.

But more than anything else, I remember Genie, my hero, my leader, my brother and best friend, Genie who knew everything about everything and chose to share it with me.

I believe most youngsters, given the chance, will develop a quest, a life's mission, if not in their mind, then certainly within their heart. Genie's quest was the world and the universe beyond. Genie loved life and the process of growing up; he loved the game; he invited the challenge; he fought a good fight. He never quit.

My quest was smaller, more clearly defined. I simply loved him.

Epilogue:

Plan "A" Completed, Sir

Many years would pass before Genie and I stood together at our Grandparent's grave, the two people who had loved us unconditionally, filling up our minds and opening our hearts with all the things every child needs to go out into the world. They understood the absolute necessity for fun; thereby creating, offering, and delivering the perfect lesson plan for life.

The sky was wonderfully blue the day we drove through the iron gates of Odd-fellow's Cemetery, where our Grandparents had been laid to rest. The clouds, like angels, hovered low, displaying their enchantments. How many summer days had we lain in the grass looking up into those marvelous paintings? How many tall ships with massive canvases did we note gliding into Heaven?

We were no longer children, but we remained Genie and Janny. We walked hand in hand among the cool, granite stone, marking stranger's lives precious to those who loved them. When we at last came to our Grandparent's grave, Genie knelt down and reached into his jacket pocket, bringing forth a small, flawless bouquet of deep purple violets, along with several sprigs of lily-of-the-valley. I sank to my knees and watched him place the flowers on the grave.

"I didn't know you knew about the violets and the lily-of-the-valley, Genie. It was Grandma's secret."

"I knew," he said softly.

Of course, he knew; Genie knew everything about everything. I asked, "Do you know the reason Grandma chose the violets and the lily-of-the-valley as the only flowers to be pressed in her family Bible?"

Genie thought for a moment and replied, "She once told me she liked violets because they were not showy; they tended to hide themselves in tall grasses. But more than their modesty, she said they were a reminder of how quickly life passes, sweet like youth, then gone. As for the lily-of-the-valley, it simply means 'Return to Happiness.'"

I couldn't speak. I nodded, took his hand, and leaned my head forward against his chest. I wanted to catch the loving beat of his heart, the soft heart he saved for me.

Walking slowly back to the car, each in our own thoughts, I suddenly said, "You know, Genie, Grandma told me you were one of God's most favored."

Genie did not reply. I couldn't read his eye and was afraid I had offended him. Then, without any warning, he let go of my hand and in his best military-command voice, shouted, "ATTENTION!"

I immediately sucked in my belly, straightened my shoulders, stuck out my chin, and gave a perfect snap-to salute. "Yes, Sir, Captain, Sir."

"Corporal Hall, are you telling me you believe, without a question, the words of a beloved, dying old lady who happened to be our Grandmother?"

"Yes, Sir, that's exactly what I'm saying."

"Forget it, Corporal. It's stuff and nonsense and extremely prejudiced from a filial point of view. Delete it; get rid of it; ignore it."

"Sorry, Sir, I cannot obey your order."

"Can't, or won't, Corporal Hall?"

"Actually, a bit of both, Sir."

"I see. Is there anything I can say or do to convince you to think otherwise?"

"No, Sir." I could see my Captain was trying hard not to smile.

Finally, gritting his teeth, he roared, "Carry on, Corporal Hall. Carry on."

"Yes, Sir," I replied smartly. "Orders, Sir?"

"Burger and fries, Corporal?"

"Yes, Sir, mighty fine, Sir."

"Good. Follow me, Corporal Hall."

"Haven't I always?" I asked.

"What was that, Corporal?"

"Nothing, Sir, just clearing my throat."

"Alright then, now, listen up, troops: FORWARD, all you choir-singin', angel-wingin', victory-bringin', favorite sons of God, MARCH!"

Afterword

Our Grandparents taught us many valuable lessons. We learned by their daily example and by their listening hearts. For me, the farm was nature walks with Grandma and experiencing the unique life lessons she lovingly taught, never tiring of my company.

For Genie, the farm was a major steppingstone into the vast world he would one day seek to conquer. But those brief, miraculous summers were a safe haven beyond the stars of our imaginations, a place forever dear and comforting as an April rain.

The farm in winter changed: the familiar paths, now celestial white, could no longer be seen. We found ourselves in a curious other world in which we had to find our own way. Challenged to move forward, we choose our direction, hoping against hope that our choice had come from the spoken and unspoken knowledge of each and every truehearted day spent on the farm, 40 acres that captured the joyous immortality of childhood.

Our Grandparents asked us to believe in what we could not see, to revel in life as a child revels in play, to honor each other with love and respect, and to mourn those who no longer heard the call of spring. But more than anything, our Grandparents taught Genie and me to remember . . .everything . . . .

Dear Genie,

> When my life is through
>
> And the angels ask me to recall
>
> The thrill of it all,
>
> I will tell them . . .I remember you.

Lyrics by Johnny Mercer

Heartstrings by Janny

Dewey Eugene Hall

February 17, 1932-January 26, 2005

Acknowledgments

Special thanks go to the Johnny Mercer Society for copyright assistance and Christine De Poortere, Peter Pan Director, of the Great Ormond Street Hospital Children's Charity, London, for her support with Peter Pan's song lyrics.

To Danielle DeConcilio, friend, typist, and editor, I thank you for traveling through the corn fields and starry sky with my brother and me. To Betty Wright, for sharing your expert knowledge of the writing craft, I give you much gratitude. To my loyal friend for over 30 years, my deepest thanks.

Tina Hagstrom, friend and illustrator, graphic artist, muralmaker, woodcutter, and artist extraordinaire. Thank you for bringing my past back to life with your beautiful work.

Above all to my beloved husband, my beloved "Frog," Buzz: you are my love and my friend . . .thank you for believing in me and encouraging me to be all I could ever hope to be.

Made in the USA
Lexington, KY
26 September 2011